IBM Cognos Business Intelligence 10.1 Dashboarding Cookbook

Working with dashboards in IBM Cognos BI 10.1:
Design, distribute, and collaborate

Ankit Garg

BIRMINGHAM - MUMBAI

IBM Cognos Business Intelligence 10.1 Dashboarding Cookbook

First published: July 2012

Production Reference: 1120712

Published by Packt Publishing Ltd.
Livery Place
35 Livery Street
Birmingham B3 2PB, UK.

ISBN 978-1-84968-582-5

www.packtpub.com

Cover Image by Asher Wishkerman (a.wishkerman@mpic.de)

Credits

Author
Ankit Garg

Reviewers
Darshan Donni
James D. Miller
Sameer Sheth

Acquisition Editor
Dilip Venkatesh

Development Editor
Unnati Shah

Technical Editor
Devdutt Kulkarni

Project Coordinator
Yashodhan Dere

Proofreader
Elinor Perry-Smith

Indexer
Rekha Nair

Production Coordinator
Shantanu Zagade

Cover Work
Shantanu Zagade

About the Author

Ankit Garg has worked in the **Business Intelligence (BI)** and **Data Warehousing (DW)** industry for the last nine years and has extensive experience with some of the challenging aspects of this industry.

Being the author of a few technical blogs and a contributor to technical forums, he has gained skills in DW, planning and budgeting, ETL, BI, and dimensional modeling.

He has authored a book—*IBM Cognos TM1 Cookbook, Packt Publishing*—on IBM Cognos TM1 9.5.X previously, and this is his second publication.

He believes in the continuous learning of new technologies and features within the industry, and sharing knowledge for mutual benefit.

I would like to dedicate this book to my family and friends, for their continuous encouragement and appreciation.

About the Reviewers

Darshan Donni has worked with the Cognos BI third-level support team for IBM India Software Labs. Prior to this, he worked with the Cognos BI second-level support team for Cognizant Technology Solutions.

He blogs actively on `http://cognoscommentary.blogspot.com`. He has participated in numerous customer engagements for IBM clients.

James D. Miller is an accomplished Senior Project Leader, Application/Systems Architect and Developer. He is an IBM Certified Professional with over 30 years of extensive experience in BI, web architecture and design, systems analysis, GUI design and testing, database modeling. He is also well-versed with systems utilizing IBM Cognos TM1 (including TM1 rules, TI, and TM1 web planning and management), dynaSight – ArcPlan, ASP, DHTML, XML, IIS, MS Visual Basic and VBA, Visual Studio, Perl, WebSuite, MS SQL Server, Oracle, Sybase SQL Server, and so on.

His responsibilities comprise of working on all aspects of Windows and SQL solution development and design. They include analysis; GUI (and website) design; data modeling; table, screen/form, and script development; SQL (and remote stored procedures and triggers) development and testing; test preparation; and management and training of programming staff.

His other experience includes the development of ETL infrastructures, such as data transfer automation between mainframe (DB2, Lawson, Great Plains, and so on) systems and SQL Client/Server, web-based applications, and the integration of enterprise applications and data sources. In addition, James has acted as Internet Applications Development Manager, responsible for the design, development, QA, and delivery of multiple websites, including online-trading applications, warehouse process control and scheduling systems, and administrative and control applications. He was also responsible for the design, development, and administration of a web-based, financial-reporting system for a 450-million dollar organization, reporting directly to the CFO and his executive team.

James has also been responsible for managing and directing multiple resources in various management roles, including Project and Team Leader, Lead Developer, and Applications Development Director. His specialties include Cognos/TM1 design and development, OLAP, Visual Basic, SQL Server, forecasting and planning, international application development, BI, and project development. His certifications include IBM Certified Developer – Cognos TM1 (he scored a perfect 100 percent on his exam) and IBM Certified Business Analyst – Cognos TM1.

James has authored the recently published book, *IBM Cognos TM1 Developer's Certification guide, Packt Publishing*.

I would sincerely like to thank my wife, Nanette, for a lifetime of endless patience, love, and support.

Sameer Sheth has been practicing as a Business Intelligence and Data Warehousing Consultant since the year 2004. His primary focus is on architectural design, development and implementation of Enterprise Performance Management, and Business Intelligence and Data Warehousing Solutions across the oil and gas, education, retail, financial, health care, and airline industries.

Overall, he has more than 13 years of relevant experience in the IT industry, blended with proven project management skills. His key roles have been as Senior Implementation Lead, Senior Solution Architect, and Project Manager. He has also spent time as Technical Mentor.

Sameer is certified in Global Business Leadership from Harvard Business School, USA. Along with this, he is certified in Managerial Excellence from Duke University's Fuqua School of Business, USA. He has numerous IBM certifications, including IBM Certified Solution Designer – Cognos 10 Planning, IBM Certified Solution Expert – Cognos 8 Planning, and IBM Certified Solution Designer – Cognos 8 Planning.

Sameer has been a Technical Reviewer for the book, *IBM Cognos TM1 Developer's Certification guide, Packt Publishing*. This book was developed to help a user master the COG-310 certification, by using an example-driven method, which was easy to understand.

Heartfelt thanks to three very special people—Shruthi, Sandeep, and Meena—each of whom, in their own way, contributed and supported me, and therefore this book.

www.PacktPub.com

Support files, eBooks, discount offers, and more

You might want to visit www.PacktPub.com for support files and downloads related to your book.

Did you know that Packt offers eBook versions of every book published, with PDF and ePub files available? You can upgrade to the eBook version at www.PacktPub.com and as a print book customer, you are entitled to a discount on the eBook copy. Get in touch with us at service@packtpub.com for more details.

At www.PacktPub.com, you can also read a collection of free technical articles, sign up for a range of free newsletters and receive exclusive discounts and offers on Packt books and eBooks.

http://PacktLib.PacktPub.com

Do you need instant solutions to your IT questions? PacktLib is Packt's online digital book library. Here, you can access, read and search across Packt's entire library of books.

Why Subscribe?

- ▶ Fully searchable across every book published by Packt
- ▶ Copy and paste, print, and bookmark content
- ▶ On demand and accessible via web browser

Free Access for Packt account holders

If you have an account with Packt at www.PacktPub.com, you can use this to access PacktLib today and view nine entirely free books. Simply use your login credentials for immediate access.

Instant Updates on New Packt Books

Get notified! Find out when new books are published by following @PacktEnterprise on Twitter, or the *Packt Enterprise* Facebook page.

Table of Contents

Preface

This book covers, in detail, the various aspects of dashboard creation and use, in IBM Cognos 10 BI.

It includes detailed information and documentation about the tools available in IBM Cognos 10 BI to show users how to create dashboards and distribute them within an organization.

Step-by-step practical recipes are included, well supported by screenshots, which makes the learning process easy, intuitive, and interesting.

This book will enable novice IBM Cognos 10 BI users to understand and exploit, in depth, the features of the product, so that they can create professional-looking dashboards and follow best industry practices, at the same time.

What this book covers

Chapter 1, IBM Cognos 10 Dashboard Components, introduces IBM Cognos 10 BI and its components. Cognos Connection, Business Insight, and Business Insight Advanced are touched upon as the primary dashboard tools provided with IBM Cognos 10 BI.

Chapter 2, Business Insight Dashboards, explores IBM Cognos Business Insight in terms of its functionality and basic layout components. This chapter focuses on explaining various navigation- and functionality-related tools available on the Business Insight interface.

Chapter 3, Business Insight Advanced Dashboard, explores IBM Cognos Business Insight Advanced in terms of its functionality and basic layout components. This chapter focuses on explaining various navigation- and functionality-related tools available on the Business Insight Advanced interface.

Chapter 4, Creating Dashboards in IBM Cognos Business Insight Advanced, includes recipes for creating the first dashboard in Business Insight Advanced. This also covers various features and functionalities in detail.

Chapter 5, Creating Dashboards in Cognos Business Insight, includes recipes for creating the first dashboard in Business Insight. This also covers various features and functionalities in detail.

Chapter 6, Sharing and Collaborating with Other Users, covers various features, using which users can share, communicate, and collaborate among themselves, and with external sources.

What you need for this book

The following software is needed for this book:

- ▸ IBM Cognos 10.1 BI
- ▸ IBM Cognos 10.1 BI Samples

Basic skills in Cognos BI are desirable for understanding the concepts of metadata packages and reports, though it is not absolutely required, as the step-by-step recipes are augmented with many screenshots and detailed descriptions, wherever needed.

Who this book is for

This book is intended for users who want to design and distribute professional-looking dashboards using IBM Cognos 10 BI, in accordance with the industry's best practices. IBM Cognos 10 BI is the market leader in providing dashboard solutions to the industry. This book delivers the information primarily using step-by-step recipes, well augmented with screenshots and theory.

Conventions

In this book, you will find a number of styles of text that distinguish between different kinds of information. Here are some examples of these styles, and an explanation of their meaning.

Code words in text are shown as follows: "Install and configure the GO Sales and GO Data Warehouse samples."

New terms and **important words** are shown in bold. Words that you see on the screen, in menus or dialog boxes for example, appear in the text like this: "Navigate to **Public Folders | Samples | Models | Interactive Samples**, as shown in the following screenshot".

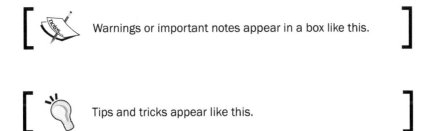

[Warnings or important notes appear in a box like this.]

[Tips and tricks appear like this.]

Reader feedback

Feedback from our readers is always welcome. Let us know what you think about this book—what you liked or may have disliked. Reader feedback is important for us to develop titles that you really get the most out of.

To send us general feedback, simply send an e-mail to feedback@packtpub.com, and mention the book title through the subject of your message.

If there is a topic that you have expertise in and you are interested in either writing or contributing to a book, see our author guide on www.packtpub.com/authors.

Customer support

Now that you are the proud owner of a Packt book, we have a number of things to help you to get the most from your purchase.

Errata

Although we have taken every care to ensure the accuracy of our content, mistakes do happen. If you find a mistake in one of our books—maybe a mistake in the text or the code—we would be grateful if you would report this to us. By doing so, you can save other readers from frustration and help us improve subsequent versions of this book. If you find any errata, please report them by visiting http://www.packtpub.com/support, selecting your book, clicking on the **errata submission form** link, and entering the details of your errata. Once your errata are verified, your submission will be accepted and the errata will be uploaded to our website, or added to any list of existing errata, under the Errata section of that title.

Piracy

Piracy of copyright material on the Internet is an ongoing problem across all media. At Packt, we take the protection of our copyright and licenses very seriously. If you come across any illegal copies of our works, in any form, on the Internet, please provide us with the location address or website name immediately so that we can pursue a remedy.

Please contact us at `copyright@packtpub.com` with a link to the suspected pirated material.

We appreciate your help in protecting our authors, and our ability to bring you valuable content.

Questions

You can contact us at `questions@packtpub.com` if you are having a problem with any aspect of the book, and we will do our best to address it.

1
IBM Cognos 10 Dashboard Components

In this chapter we will be:

- ▶ Introducing IBM Cognos 10 BI Cognos Connection
- ▶ Exploring IBM Cognos Business Insight User Interface
- ▶ Exploring IBM Cognos Business Insight Advanced User Interface

Introduction

IBM Cognos 10 BI is the leading performance management tool, which enables users to monitor, measure, and manage corporate performance at a glance.

With its dashboard capabilities, users can assemble and organize data in personalized dashboard views to support different decision-making requirements.

IBM Cognos 10 BI is a bundle of tools that are accessible through a web interface and can be used for different sets of requirements. The following table briefly touches upon each of these:

IBM Cognos BI component name	Use case
Report Studio	Advanced report authoring interface where queries and calculations can be created manually. User needs to have BI designer skills.
Analysis Studio	Interface to perform dimensional data analysis where an analyst can slice and dice data stored in the multidimensional format.
Query Studio	Business users can perform ad hoc data analysis. Simple queries are generated on the fly.
Event Studio	Used to managing data related situations and triggering actions based on specific data conditions.
Business Insight	Users can use existing components to assemble and distribute sophisticated dashboards.
Business Insight Advanced	Business users can author reports and dashboards in a way similar to Report Studio, but with much less complexity. Queries are generated on the fly and no manual creation of queries is required. It provides functionality that is a subset of Report Studio with an intuitive and easy user interface.

IBM Cognos 10 BI has introduced IBM Cognos Business Insight and IBM Cognos Business Insight Advanced, which are the two components that can be used to author and view dashboards.

IBM Cognos Business Insight is used to create sophisticated interactive dashboards from the existing content. For instance, assume a user has already created four different reports each catering to sales, marketing, HR, and finance, using Report Studio. Individual sections in these reports can then be used in IBM Cognos Business Insight independently, to create an interactive dashboard. This would mean that the dashboard can have a few charts from the first two reports, and a list and a crosstab from third and fourth reports respectively.

IBM Cognos Business Insight Advanced is used to perform deeper analysis and report authoring where a user can perform more advanced data exploration, such as adding additional measures, conditional formatting, and advanced calculations. This can be thought of as a clipped version of IBM Cognos Report Studio, which is a complex report authoring tool in which queries and calculations can be built.

In this book we will be covering various aspects of IBM Cognos 10 Business Insight and IBM Cognos 10 Business Insight Advanced.

Readers are advised to install and configure IBM Cognos 10 BI and Samples (GO Sales and GO Data Warehouse), provided with the tool installation kit. For detailed installation and configuration instructions, please refer to IBM Cognos 10 BI Installation and Configuration Guide, shipped with the product.

Introducing IBM Cognos 10 BI Cognos Connection

In this recipe we will be exploring Cognos Connection, which is the user interface presented to the user when he/she logs in to IBM Cognos 10 BI for the first time.

> IBM Cognos 10 BI, once installed and configured, can be accessed through the Web using supported web browsers. For a list of supported web browsers, refer to the Installation and Configuration Guide shipped with the product.

Getting ready

As stated earlier, make sure that IBM Cognos 10 BI is installed and configured. Install and configure the GO Sales and GO Data Warehouse samples. Use the gateway URI to log on to the web interface called Cognos Connection.

How to do it...

To explore Cognos Connection, perform the following steps:

1. Log on to Cognos Connection using the gateway URI that may be similar to `http://<HostName>:<PortNumber>/ibmcognos/cgi-bin/cognos.cgi`.

2. Take note of the Cognos Connection interface. It has the **GO Sales** and **GO Data Warehouse** samples visible.

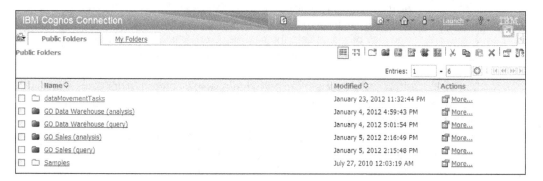

3. Note the blue-coloured folder icon, shown as in the preceding screenshot. It represents metadata model packages that are published to Cognos Connection using the Cognos Framework Manager tool. These packages have objects that represent business data objects, relationships, and calculations, which can be used to author reports and dashboards.

> Refer to the book, *IBM Cognos TM1 Cookbook* by Packt Publishing to learn how to create metadata models packages.

4. From the toolbar, click on **Launch**. This will open a menu, showing different studios, each having different functionality, as shown in the following screenshot:

5. We will use **Business Insight** and **Business Insight Advanced**, which are the first two choices in the preceding menu. These are the two components used to create and view dashboards.

> For other options, refer to the corresponding books by the same publisher. For instance, refer to the book, *IBM Cognos 8 Report Studio Cookbook* to know more about creating and distributing complex reports. Query Studio and Analysis Studio are meant to provide business users with the facility to slice and dice business data themselves. Event Studio is meant to define business situations and corresponding actions.

6. Coming back to Cognos Connection, note that a yellow-colored folder icon, which is shown as represents a user-defined folder, which may or may not contain other published metadata model packages, reports, dashboards, and other content. In our case, we have a user-defined folder called **Samples**. This was created when we installed and configured samples shipped with the product.

Click on the **New Folder** icon, which is represented by , on the toolbar to create a user-defined folder. Other options are also visible here, for instance to create a new dashboard.

7. Click on the user-defined folder—**Samples** to view its contents, as shown in the following screenshot:

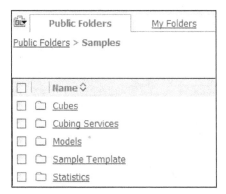

8. As shown in the preceding screenshot, it has more such folders, each having its own content. The top part of the pane shows the navigation path. Let's navigate deeper into **Models | Business Insight Samples** to show some sample dashboards, created using IBM Cognos Business Insight, as shown in the following screenshot:

9. Click on one of these links to view the corresponding dashboard. For instance, click on **Sales Dashboard (Interactive)** to view the dashboard, as shown in the following screenshot:

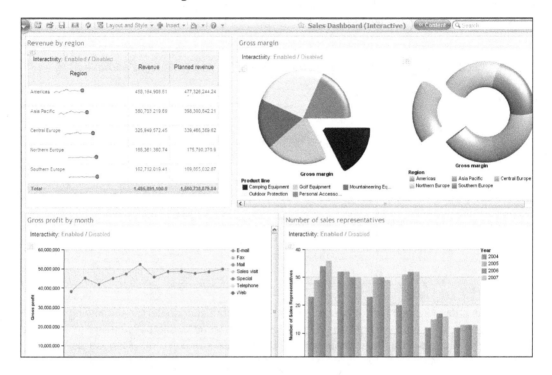

10. The dashboard can also be opened in the authoring tool, which is IBM Cognos Business Insight, in this case by clicking on the icon shown as 🖼 on extreme right, on Cognos Connection. It will show the same result as shown in the preceding screenshot.

11. We will see the Business Insight interface in detail later in this chapter.

How it works...

Cognos Connection is the primary user interface that user sees when he/she logs in for the first time. Business data has to be first identified and imported from the metadata model using the Cognos Framework Manager tool. Relationships (inner/outer joins) and calculations are then created, and the resultant metadata model package is published to the IBM Cognos 10 BI Server. This becomes available on Cognos Connection. Users are given access to appropriate studios on Cognos Connection, according to their needs. Analysis, reports, and dashboards are then created and distributed using one of these studios. The preceding sample has used Business Insight, for instance.

Later sections in this chapter will look more into Business Insight and Business Insight Advanced. The next section focuses on the Business Insight interface details from the navigation perspective.

Exploring IBM Cognos Business Insight User Interface

In this recipe we will explore IBM Cognos Business Insight User Interface in more detail. We will explore various areas of the UI, each dedicated to perform different actions.

Getting ready

As stated earlier, we will be exploring different sections of Cognos Business Insight. Hence, make sure that IBM Cognos 10 BI installation is open and samples are set up properly. We will start the recipe assuming that the **IBM Cognos Connection** window is already open on the screen.

How to do it...

To explore IBM Cognos Business Insight User Interface, perform the following steps:

1. In the **IBM Cognos Connection** window, navigate to **Business Insight Samples**, as shown in the following screenshot:

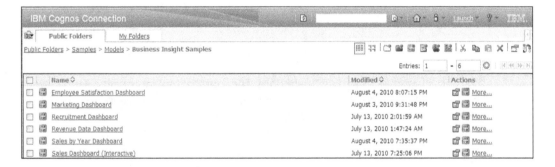

2. Click on one of the dashboards, for instance **Marketing Dashboard** to open the dashboard in Business Insight. Different areas are labeled, as shown in the following figure:

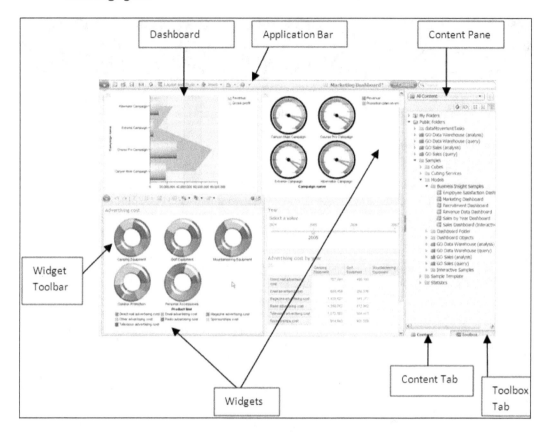

3. The overall layout is termed as **Dashboard**. The topmost toolbar is called **Application bar**. The Application bar contains different icons to manage the dashboard as a whole. For instance, we can create, open, e-mail, share, or save the dashboard using one of the icons on the Application bar.

The user can explore different icons on the Application bar by hovering the mouse pointer over them. Hovering displays the tooltip, which has a brief but self-explanatory help text.

4. Similarly, it has a **Widget toolbar** for every widget, which gets activated when the user clicks on the corresponding widget. When the mouse is focused away from the widget, the Widget toolbar disappears. It has various options, for instance to refresh the widget data, print as PDF, resize to fit content, and so on. It also provides the user with the capability to change the chart type as well as to change the color palette. We will see each of these options in detail when we visit *Chapter 2, Business Insight Dashboards*. However, all these options have help text associated with them, which is activated on mouse hover.

5. **Content tab** and **Content pane** show the list of objects available on the Cognos Connection. Directory structure on Cognos Connection can be navigated using Content pane and Content tab, and hence, available objects can be added to or removed from the dashboard. The drag-and-drop functionality has been provided as a result of which creating and editing a dashboard has become as simple as moving objects between the Dashboard area and Cognos Connection.

6. The **Toolbox tab** displays additional widgets. The **Slider Filter** and **Select Value Filter** widgets allow the user to filter report content. The other toolbox widgets allow user to add more report content to the dashboard, such as HTML content, images, RSS feeds, and rich text. We will see all these in more detail when we visit *Chapter 2, Business Insight Dashboards*.

How it works...

In the preceding section, we have seen basic areas of Business Insight. More than one user can log on to the IBM Cognos 10 BI server, and create various objects on Cognos Connection. These objects include packages, reports, cubes, templates, and statistics to name a few.

These objects can be created using one or more tools available to users. For instance, reports can be created using one of the studios available. Cubes can be created using IBM Cognos TM1 or IBM Cognos Transformer and published on Cognos Connection. Metadata model packages can be created using IBM Cognos Framework Manager and published on Cognos Connection.

These objects can then be dragged, dropped, and formatted as standalone objects in Cognos Business Insight, and hence, dashboards can be created.

The next chapter will explore Cognos Business Insight in more detail and we will actually be exploring the whole idea of creating dashboards using Business Insight and Business Insight Advanced, more deeply.

Exploring IBM Cognos Business Insight Advanced User Interface

In this recipe, we will go through the basic user interface provided with IBM Cognos Business Insight Advanced.

Getting ready

A working IBM Cognos 10 BI setup is necessary for this recipe. Install and configure the GO Sales and GO Data Warehouse samples shipped with the product.

How to do it...

To explore IBM Cognos Business Insight Advanced User Interface, perform the following steps:

1. Navigate to Cognos Connection using the URI, as stated earlier.

2. Navigate to **Public Folders** | **Samples** | **Models** | **Interactive Samples**, as shown in the following screenshot:

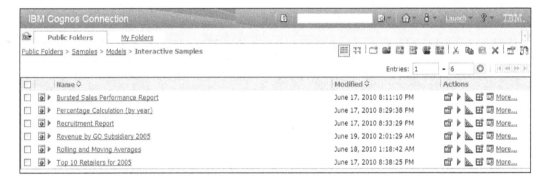

3. Click on the More... icon on the extreme right of the **Top 10 Retailers for 2005** entry. It will show multiple actions that can be performed on the report entry. Click on the **Open with Business Insight Advanced** option to open the report in Business Insight Advanced.

4. By clicking on the icon, it will open the report in Cognos Report Studio. This report has been created using Cognos Report Studio, which is evident from the icon besides the report name. We want to open this report in Cognos Business Insight Advanced, hence we have clicked on the **More...** icon.

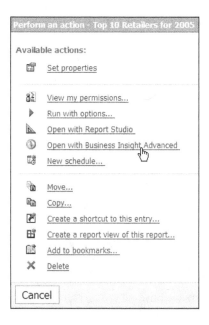

5. This will open the report in Business Insight Advanced, as shown in the following figure. Important sections are labeled accordingly:

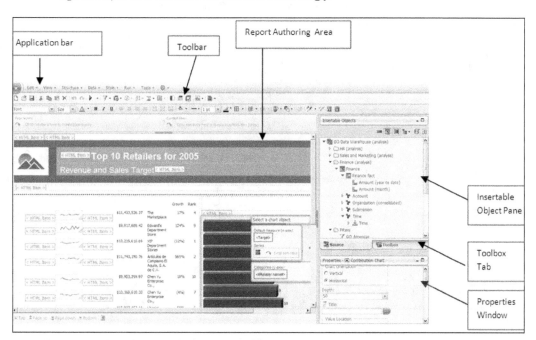

6. The **Application bar** area contains options to manage reports (for instance to create, open, and save a report). General options, for instance to cut, copy, paste, and delete are also provided in the same area. Specific options, which help the user to author and modify reports, are also present in the Application bar area. The same options are provided as icons on **Toolbar**.

Hover the mouse pointer over any of these options to display help text, which is self-explanatory and intuitive.

7. The **Insertable Objects pane** displays the metadata model package used to author the report. Components can be dragged-and-dropped from the package to the **Report Authoring area**.

8. The **Toolbox tab** has a list of static objects, which can be used to format the report in a certain way. For instance, a crosstab can be selected, dragged, and dropped to the Report Authoring area to build on the layout of the report.

9. The **Properties window** displays all the properties of the object that is currently selected in the Report Authoring area. The user can change properties of the report objects as required.

10. Click on the ▶ icon from the Toolbar area to execute the report. The report will be rendered as HTML, in a new window called **IBM Cognos Viewer**, as shown in the following screenshot:

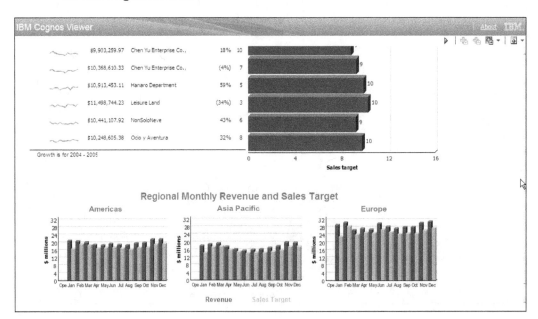

11. Dashboard pages can be designed so that URIs of such reports can be placed in the left-hand side pane. Configurations can be done to display the corresponding output on the right-hand side pane if a user clicks on the corresponding URI on the left-hand side pane.

12. Such reports can also be directly used while creating dashboards in Cognos Business Insight.

How it works...

Cognos Report Studio has a similar interface to the preceding one, but is used to author more complex reports. Such reports created using Business Insight Advanced and Report Studio can be saved on Cognos Connection. These reports can be distributed to users as dashboards or as management reports.

Individual objects defined in these reports can be used independently in Business Insight to create more sophisticated dashboards. The advantage of such dashboards is that the summary data from various domains and functional areas, which is ready to be viewed in a user-friendly manner, can be collected and presented to users as one executive dashboard.

Going forward, we will focus more on creating the dashboards in the most efficient ways. Tips and relevant information about other related components will be shared throughout the book as and when required.

The next chapter will focus on Cognos Business Insight and some of the best practices in presenting business data to business users.

2
Business Insight Dashboards

In this chapter we will be:

- ▸ Opening a dashboard in IBM Cognos Business Insight
- ▸ Exploring the Content and Toolbox panes, and customizing the dashboard view
- ▸ Exploring widget controls and customizing widgets
- ▸ Exploring the Application bar

Introduction

In this chapter we will view existing dashboards in IBM Cognos 10 Business Insight. We have already seen different sections in the IBM Cognos Business Insight UI. We will learn how we can interact with dashboards in IBM Cognos Business Insight from a user perspective.

Opening a dashboard in IBM Cognos Business Insight

In this recipe we will open an existing dashboard. We will use samples provided with the IBM Cognos 10 BI setup.

Getting ready

IBM Cognos 10 BI Server should be up and the GO Sales and GO Data Warehouse samples should be installed and configured.

How to do it...

To open a dashboard in IBM Cognos Business Insight, perform the following steps:

1. Open Cognos Connection, using the gateway URI in a web browser. Navigate to **Business Insight Samples**, as shown in the following screenshot:

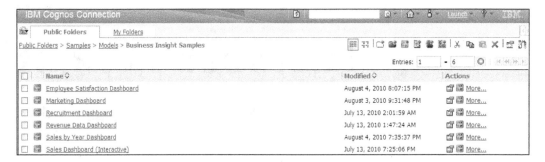

2. Click on **Recruitment Dashboard**, which is the third entry in the screenshot. This will open the dashboard in Cognos Business Insight, as shown in the following screenshot:

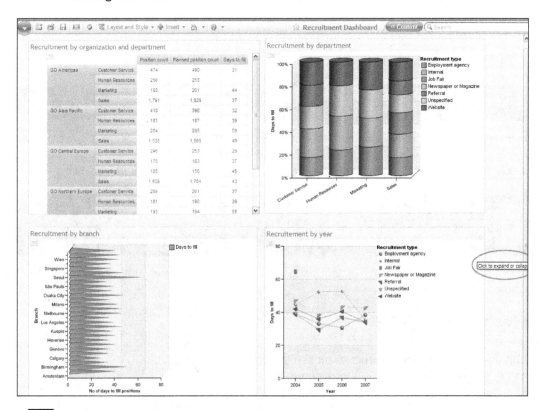

3. The preceding dashboard is the collection of a crosstab and three charts. We will focus on each of the areas one by one in the next recipes. Take note of the rightmost area circled in red. It indicates that the section is collapsible. This is the subject of discussion for the next recipe.

How it works...

In this recipe we have used existing dashboards as part of the samples available with IBM Cognos 10 BI setup. The user is able to navigate to the dashboard through Cognos Connection. Clicking on the dashboard will open it, showing the latest data. Data is sourced from data source connections, already configured while installing the `GO Sales` and `GO Data Warehouse` samples.

The next section will focus on Cognos Business Insight in detail. We have already discussed this briefly in the previous chapter. Now we will analyze it in more detail.

Exploring the Content and Toolbox panes, and customizing the dashboard view

In the previous recipe we showed a vertical collapsible section, circled in red. Clicking on this section will open the Content and Toolbox panes, which we will see in detail now.

Getting ready

We will continue from where we left off in the previous section. We will click on the red-circled area on **Recruitment Dashboard** and analyze the Content pane first.

How to do it...

To explore the Content and Toolbox panes, perform the following steps:

1. Open **Recruitment Dashboard** in the Cognos Business Insight interface.

2. Shown in the following screenshot are the **Content** and **Toolbox** tabs. These are currently in expanded mode. They can be collapsed to hide the tabs, by clicking on the █ button, which we had highlighted in the earlier recipe.

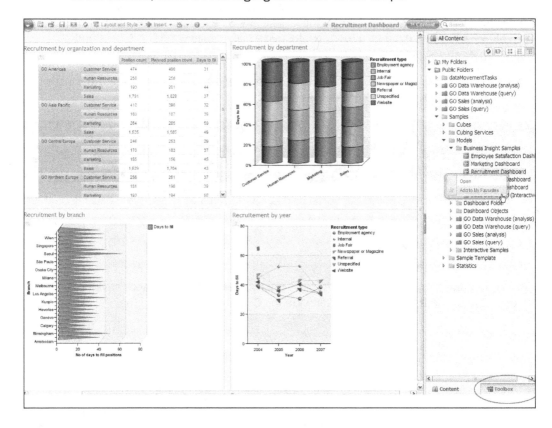

3. The Content pane can act as a navigator with which any other Cognos object can be viewed at any point in time. Any entry can be selected. Just right-click on that entry and click on the **Open** option from the menu. This will open the object in the same window. An entry can also be added to favorites by clicking on **Add to My Favorites**.

Users are advised to add all the objects they need frequently to their favorites/bookmarks in the web browser. This will save them from hassle remembering names on the Cognos Connection. This is important when you have a large number of dashboards with confusing names.

4. In the preceding screenshot, the **Toolbox** tab is circled in red. This is provided to enhance or filter data displayed on the dashboard. A user can right-click on the options listed in the **Toolbox** tab and click on **Insert**. The corresponding control on the **Toolbox** tab will be inserted and applied to the widget selected.

5. Click on the top-leftmost crosstab, which represents **Recruitment by organization and department**. This will highlight the crosstab, as shown in the following screenshot:

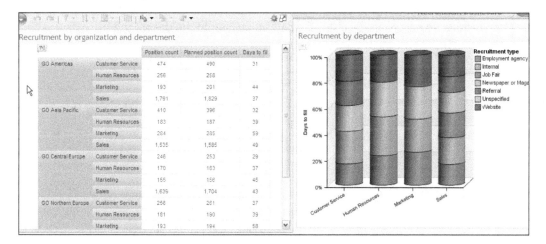

 A **widget** is a component of the interface that enables a user to perform a function or access a service. The Widget toolbar can be used to change the behavior of the widget to a certain extent.

The widget toolbar is now available on the crosstab as we have selected the widget. This toolbar is specific to the widget selected. We will see the widget toolbar in more detail later.

6. Activate the **Toolbox** tab on the rightmost side. This will open the Toolbox pane. Right-click on **Select Value Filter**. From the menu options, select **Insert**, as shown in the following screenshot:

7. This will open a pop-up window—**Properties – Select Value Filter**. We will try to filter data here and limit what is being shown in the crosstab. Have a look at the pop-up window in the following screenshot. Let us analyze the pop-up window to see what options we have while applying a select value filter to the dashboard.

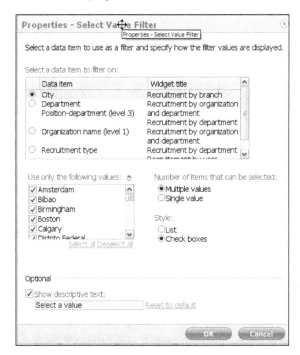

8. We can apply this filter to one of the widgets on the left-hand side Dashboard pane. **Select a data item to filter on** is the first section in the **Properties – Select Value Filter** window. Using this, a section value filter can be applied to one of the relevant data items, which is used in widgets. Hence, a data item and the corresponding widget can be selected in the section, so that the filter applies to the selected item.

9. For instance, in the preceding screenshot we want the filter to be applied to the **Recruitment by branch** widget. This is the bottom-leftmost widget, which displays **Days to fill** by branch (**City**). Underlying data item—**City** is used to display the branch, in the query.

> Do not focus on how queries are coded in IBM Cognos Business Insight. Typically, queries are created using other components of IBM Cognos 10, such as IBM Cognos Report Studio, and used directly in IBM Cognos Business Insight.

10. The second section in the **Properties – Select Value Filter** window provides the user with the ability to select one or multiple actual values, and depending on that, the appropriate style can be applied to the filter.

11. In the preceding screenshot, let us assume that we want a user to be able to select a single branch from the set of radio buttons, and hence, filter the data appearing in the widget. The following screenshot shows the corresponding settings that need to be applied. Click on **OK**, once the settings have been applied.

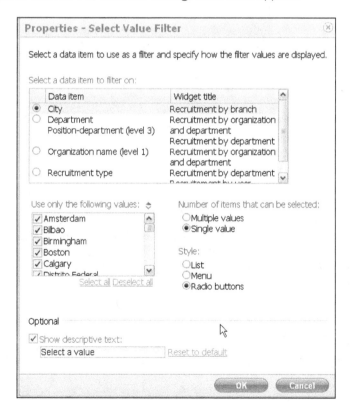

12. The third section, which is **Optional**, enables the user to provide a descriptive text with the filter, as shown in the following screenshot:

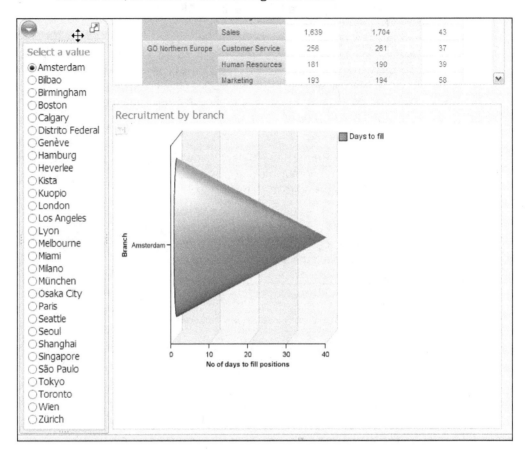

13. The additional window is the filter we have just applied. One of the values can be selected and the **Recruitment by branch** chart changes accordingly. The filter can be removed by selecting the **Remove from Dashboard** menu item, which will delete the filter altogether and the widget will return to its original state. The **Send to Back** menu option will push the filter widget to the background but it remains applicable.

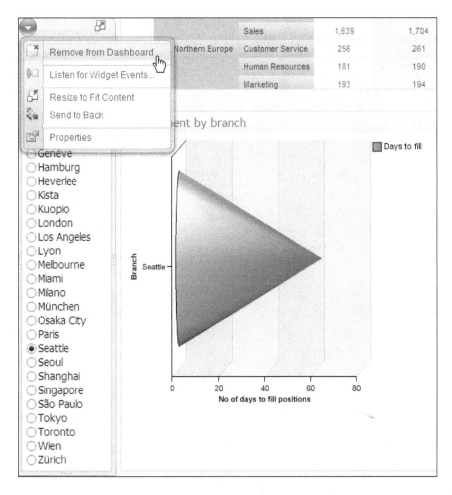

14. Clicking on **Properties** will again open the **Properties – Select Value Filter** window, which we saw earlier. It will help users to reconfigure the filter. **Resize to Fit Content** will adjust the size of the filter widget. **Listen to Widget Events** enables a user to configure one widget and change it according to the events in any other widget on the dashboard. Hence, the user can use data items used in one widget to filter data in another widget.

15. Now let us use **Remove from Dashboard** to delete the filter and return to its original state. We want to explore other options in the Toolbox pane.

16. Another similar item to explore in the Toolbox pane is **Slider Filter**, which works in similar way to **Select Value Filter**. A slider filter when inserted in the dashboard needs to be configured first, using the **Properties – A slider filter** window, as shown in the following screenshot:

17. Here we want to apply a numerical range filter on a measure data item—**Days to fill**, which is applicable to all the four widgets. The **From:** and **To:** values can be configured manually, or else these are automatically set to lowest and highest value of the data item respectively.

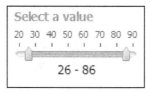

18. Let us change lower value from **26** to **50**. This will change all the four widgets as the data item—**Days to fill** is used in all the four widgets.

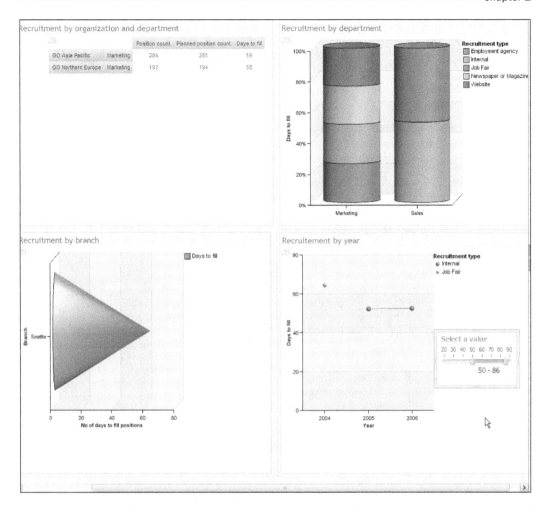

19. Similar to the slider filter, this filter can also be removed by clicking on **Remove from Dashboard**, resized by clicking on **Resize to Fit Content**, or pushed to the background by clicking on **Send to Back**.

> In order to flip-flop the filter control from front to background and vice versa, click on the filter widget and chart/crosstab/list and vice versa.

20. Let us remove **Slider Filter** to return to its original state. We will explore the remaining options in the Toolbox pane.

21. Other toolbox items such as web page, image, and text can be added to the dashboard. The user just needs to right-click and then click on **Insert** from the menu. A valid URL needs to be entered for the web page and image. The user can also configure target URL for an image to navigate to a URL when the image is clicked. Inserting text will open a text editor, so that user can format and insert required text on the dashboard.

22. The last two options are **My Inbox** and **RSS Feed**. To display e-mails relevant to the business user, mail server options need to be configured correctly while installing IBM Cognos 10 BI environment.

23. Inserting RSS feed, requires the user to specify a valid URL for the RSS or Atom feed in the **Type the URL address for the RSS or Atom feed** field. Under the **Options:** section, three options are provided such as **Show feed details**, **Show the feed icon**, and **Show alternating background**, as shown in the following screenshot:

24. Do not change anything to **Recruitment Dashboard**, and keep it in its original state.

How it works...

In this recipe we have seen how a user can enhance/filter the dashboard view and customize it according to his/her own preferences. The dashboard can then be added to favorites and the user doesn't need to navigate and search all the entries on Cognos Connection for the required dashboard.

The next recipe will zoom in to widget controls and we will see how we can customize each widget independently. Options are provided so that users can format and customize each widget independently according to his/her own preferences.

Exploring widget controls and customizing widgets

In IBM Cognos Business Insight, the user can double-click on a widget or on the dashboard, and make the Widget toolbar visible. In this recipe we will explore the Widget toolbar.

Getting ready

We will use Business Insight Samples we have been following up in previous recipes. Let us navigate to **Public Folders** | **Samples** | **Models** | **Business Insight Samples**, on IBM Cognos Connection and click on the **Marketing Dashboard** link.

How to do it...

To explore widget controls and customize widgets, perform the following steps:

1. Open **Marketing Dashboard**. As can be seen in the following screenshot, the user has clicked on the **Advertising cost** chart, which has its own toolbar highlighted and circled in red. Every widget has its own toolbar, which can be brought to the front by clicking on the corresponding widget.

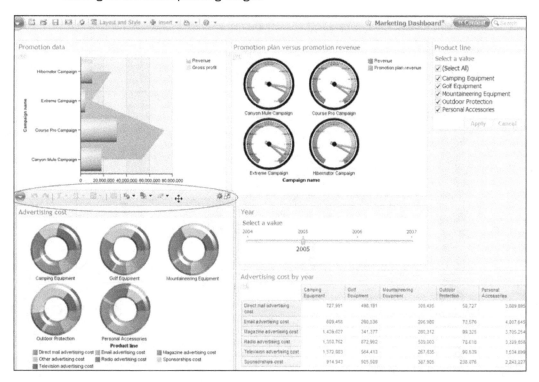

2. Let us now explore each of the options provided on the Widget toolbar.

3. Click on the **Widget Actions** icon, as shown in the following screenshot. The first menu item is **Remove from Dashboard**, which will remove the widget from the dashboard.

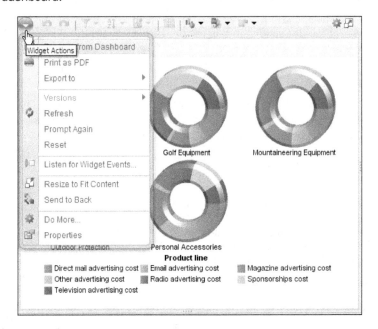

4. Next menu option—**Print as PDF** will execute the chart and render it in PDF format. This can be printed and distributed as a hard copy.

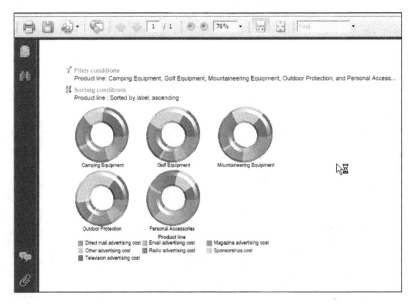

5. The widget can also be exported to other formats such as Excel 2007 and Excel 2002 using the **Export to** option.

> Exporting a chart in the CSV format will actually download corresponding data, which is used to render the chart, in the CSV format. Hence, please remember that charts when exported as CSV will not have any graphical part rendered but will only have data in tabular format as shown in the following figure. This feature will help to debug data-related issues with the chart.

	Camping Equipment	Golf Equipment	Mountaineering Equipment	Outdoor Protection	Personal Accessories
Direct mail advertising cost	2652038	1902806	1338742	138293	11361375
Email advertising cost	2186843	1112885	888998	172221	14044981
Magazine advertising cost	5139172	1286395	1201027	254106	12759384
Other advertising cost	482341	204758	183400	41037	1381607
Radio advertising cost	4915605	3285758	2165117	233862	12547660
Sponsorships cost	3305050	3304037	1659448	636677	8483116
Television advertising cost	5512110	2169131	1134726	255381	5721812

5825EN:
Chart rendered as CSV will download this output. This can be particularly useful to debug data related issues with the chart.

6. There are options provided to maintain data in the chart. Different versions of the same widget can be managed and one of them can be used on the dashboard. Versions of the widget to be used can be changed by the user by expanding the **Versions** menu option.

7. Similarly, data appearing in the chart can be refreshed by clicking on the **Refresh** option.

> The **Refresh** option is particularly useful when user wants to compare data before and after refresh. The same widget can be placed on the dashboard side-by-side. After the data feed, refresh only one of them to have new and old data side-by-side. This helps in comparing data before refresh and after refresh.

8. **Listen for Widget Events...** defines how the given widget will react to different events happening for other widgets on the dashboard. There may be a use case to drill down to a chart automatically when the user performs a drill action on another chart. This is useful to maintain the same context of information across all or more than one widget on the dashboard.

9. The size and visibility of the widget can be controlled by the next two menu options, which are **Resize to Fit Content** and **Send to Back**.

10. Clicking on **Properties** will pop up another window, which enables the user to define the title of the widget along with general properties, as shown in the following screenshot:

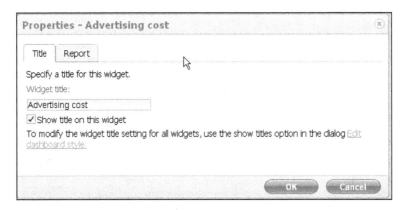

11. Take a look at the **Report** tab in the **Properties** window now:

12. The **Do More...** option is provided to open the widget in a separate interface, which has more capabilities to manipulate the data and layout of the widget. Refer to the screenshot right after the following information box for an idea as to which interface pops up when the **Do More...** option is selected for the **Advertising cost** widget on the dashboard.

The **Do More...** option gives additional actions to the user, which can be performed on the widget. A new window opens in the same window and when the user is done, he/she can click on **Cancel** or **Done** to return to the original dashboard.

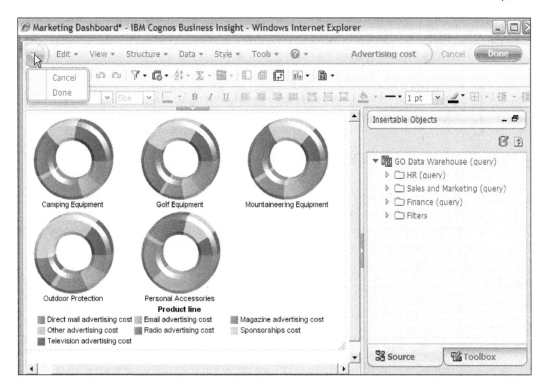

13. We will see similar interfaces to the preceding one when we discuss IBM Cognos Business Insight Advanced. Click on **Cancel** and return to the original dashboard.

14. Now we will see the rest of the Widget toolbar in detail. Refer to the following screenshot to get an idea of what we want to discuss:

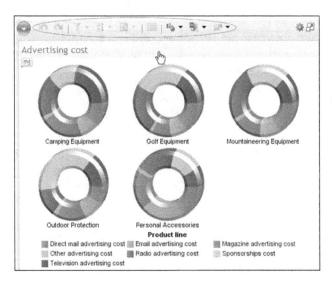

15. The first two icons denoted by , are meant for **Redo** and **Undo** changes. Their functionality is similar to what is already there in many popular word processing programs such as MS Word.

> The user can hover his/her mouse on these icons for intuitive and brief help text that comes up as a tooltip.

16. The next section on the toolbar has icons—⬜ to filter data, ⬜ to sort data, and ⬜ to insert calculations.

17. Let us have a look at the filter options first. On another widget on the same dashboard, that is, **Advertising cost by year**, double-click on the crosstab to expose the Widget toolbar. Click on the intersection between **Magazine advertising cost** and **Camping Equipment**, and expand the filter menu as shown in following screenshot:

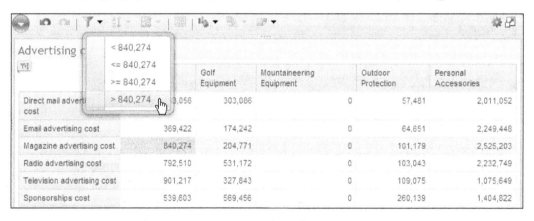

18. The user can apply four types of filters based on the cell value. Select **>840,274** to apply a filter magazine advertisement cost less than 840,274. As this is true for **Personal Accessories**, we will see the output after the filter has been applied, as shown in the following screenshot:

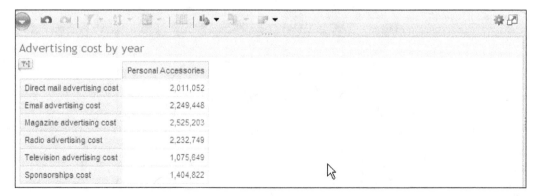

19. The ⊞ Icon can be clicked to see which filter and sort criterion has been set on that widget. Click on this icon, as shown in the following screenshot, to view the filters and sorting that are currently applicable to the **Advertising cost by year** widget.

20. Close and open the **Marketing Dashboard** window again, without saving anything. Click on the **Expand** icon, as shown in the following screenshot, for the **Advertising cost by year** widget. Note that two filters — slider filter and select value filter, have already been applied to the widget. These are same type of filters we were discussing for the Toolbox pane in the previous recipe.

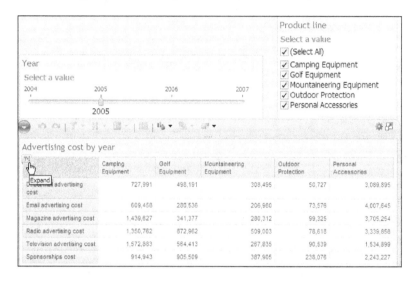

21. Clicking on the **Expand** icon will open a small area displaying current settings in terms of filers and sorting, as shown in the following screenshot:

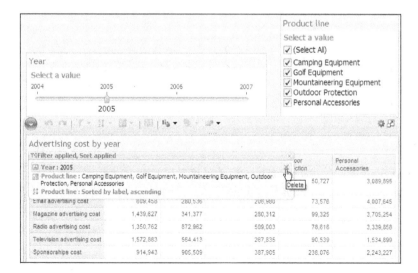

22. Take a note of the first filter, which is set using the slider filter. This can be removed by clicking on **Delete** denoted by the ✕ icon, as shown in the preceding screenshot, next to the specific filter.

23. On the same widget, click on first column that is **Camping Equipment**, click on **Sort By Label**, and select **Descending** from the menu, as shown in the following screenshot:

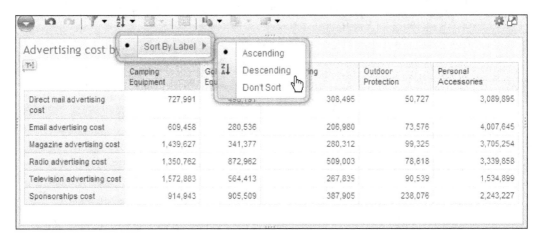

24. Note the change in the order in which columns appear:

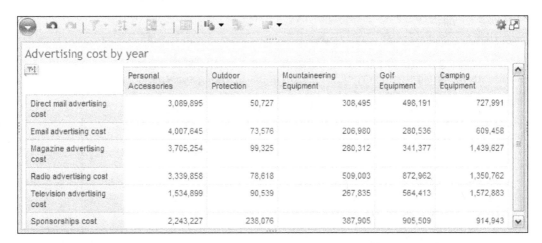

25. Newly added sort—**Product line: Sorted by label, descending** is visible in the menu, as shown in the following screenshot:

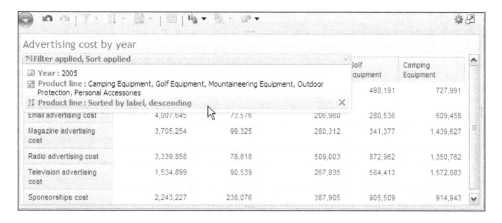

26. Changes can be reverted by clicking on the 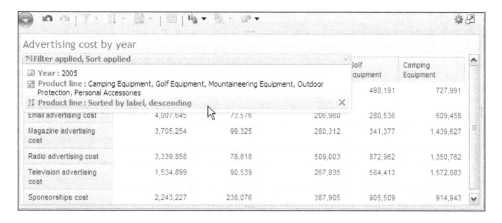 icon. Click on that to return to its original state.

27. Similarly, click on **Direct mail advertising cost row** and insert a calculation by clicking on the **Calculate** icon—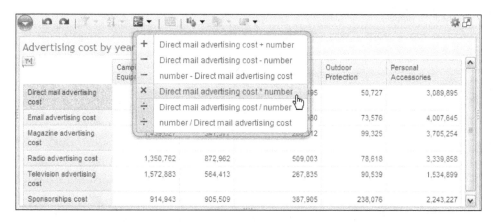. We want to insert a calculation, which has direct mail advertising cost multiplied by a static number, which is displayed as **Direct mail advertising cost * number**, as shown in the following screenshot:

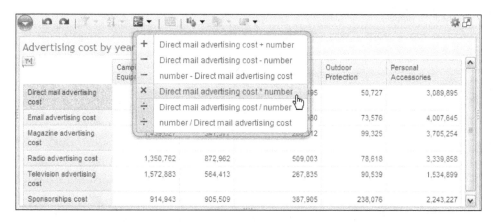

28. The **Enter the number** pop-up window is generated, as shown in the following screenshot. Enter number **10** in the **Number** field:

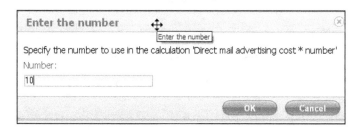

29. Note that a new row has been generated showing the calculated values, as shown in the following screenshot:

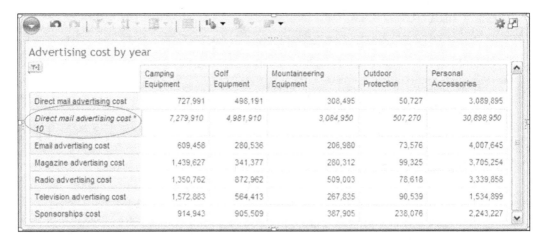

30. Close the current dashboard without saving any changes and open **Sales by Year Dashboard** from Cognos Connection, as shown in the following screenshot:

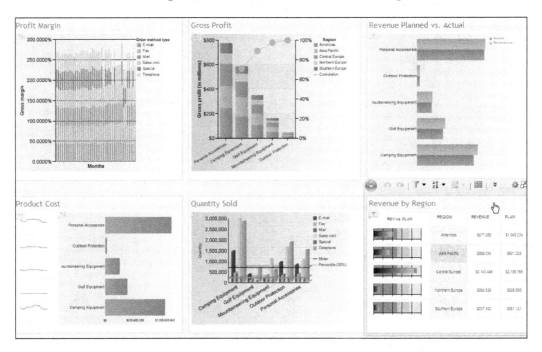

31. Click on the **Revenue by Region** widget, click on the **REGION** column and click on **Group/Ungroup** denoted by the ▦ icon from the Widget toolbar. This will apply grouping on **REGION** and the widget layout is changed, as shown in the following screenshot:

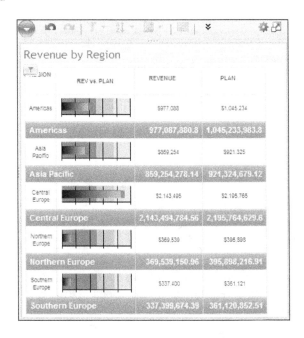

32. The same icon can be used to ungroup and the widget returns to the old state.

33. Now click on the **Revenue Planned vs. Actual** widget to expose the Widget toolbar.

34. Click on the chart and change the display type to **Pie Chart**, as shown in the following screenshot. Note that the ▦ icon is used for **Change Display Type**:

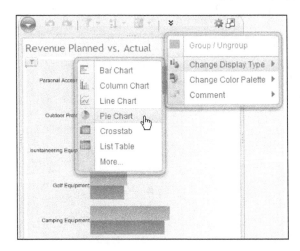

35. Note the chart layout changes to a pie chart:

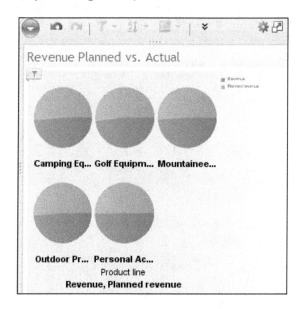

36. Similarly, we will the change color palette of the **Gross profit** widget by clicking on the **Change Color Palette** option and then selecting **Gradients**, as shown in the following screenshot:

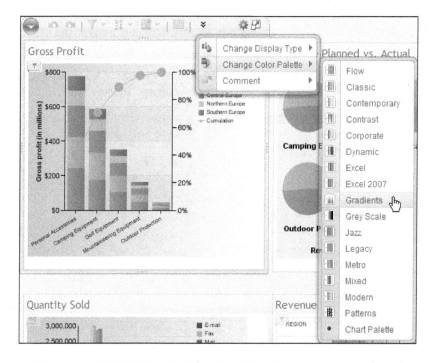

37. Note the change in the color palette, as shown in the following screenshot:

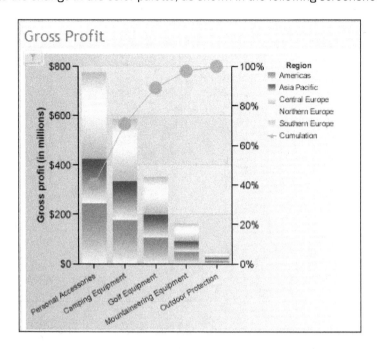

38. The user can also insert a comment by clicking on **Comment** denoted by the icon in the **Profit Margin** widget and then clicking on **Add comment – Profit margin chart**. It will open a text editor, which can be used to type comments.

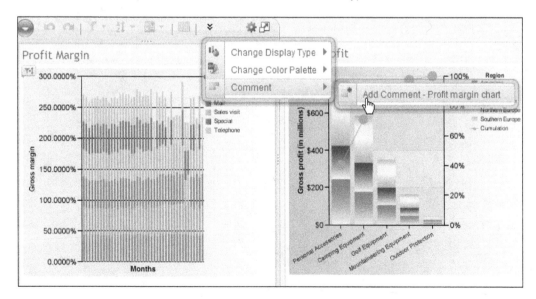

39. When inserted, these comments are displayed as a tooltip, when the mouse is hovered on the area shown in the following screenshot:

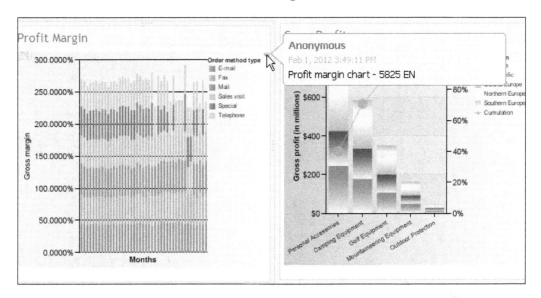

40. The same widget menu can be arrived at through selecting and right-clicking on a widget, as shown in the following screenshot:

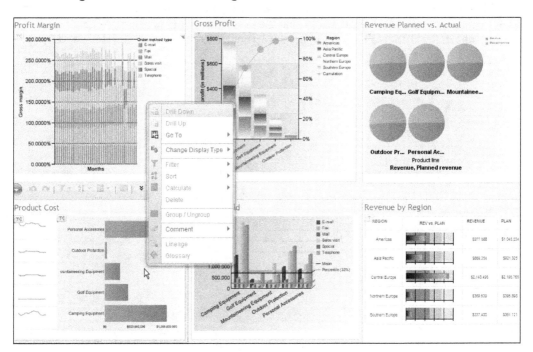

41. We will revisit the menu again in later chapters, to discuss drill functionality.

42. Close the dashboard without saving changes.

How it works...

This recipe is based on the GO Sales and GO Data Warehouse samples shipped with IBM Cognos 10 BI. The user, once logged on to a dashboard can play around with settings specific to a widget using a Widget toolbar. We have explored each option in this recipe and should now be able to explore further.

In *Chapter 4, Creating Dashboards in IBM Cognos Business Insight Advanced*, we will see how we can drill up and drill down from master view to detailed view. A separate chapter is dedicated to drill functionality, which is quite useful in making dashboards interactive.

In the next recipe we will focus on the Application bar, which is at the top of the IBM Cognos Business Insight window.

Exploring the Application bar

In this recipe we will focus on the Application bar, which is placed at the top of the IBM Cognos Business Insight window.

Getting ready

We will use the GO Sales and GO Data Warehouse samples shipped with IBM Cognos 10 BI. Ensure that IBM Cognos 10 BI Server is running and samples are set up properly.

How to do it...

To explore the Application bar, perform the following steps:

1. Open Cognos Connection and navigate to **Public Folders | Samples | Models | Business Insight Samples**.

2. Click on **Revenue Data Dashboard** to open it, as shown in the following screenshot:

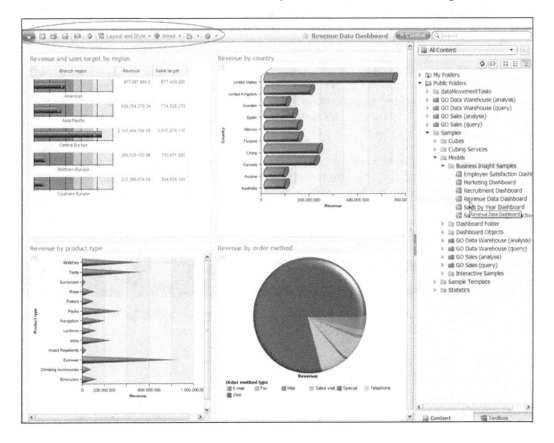

3. We will explore the region circled in the preceding screenshot. This is the Application bar, which we briefly saw in *Chapter 1, IBM Cognos 10 Dashboard Components*.

4. The top-leftmost icon has menu items, which perform various tasks with the dashboard. Users can e-mail the link of the dashboard via mailbox using the **Email Link...** option, configured while setting up the IBM Cognos BI Server.

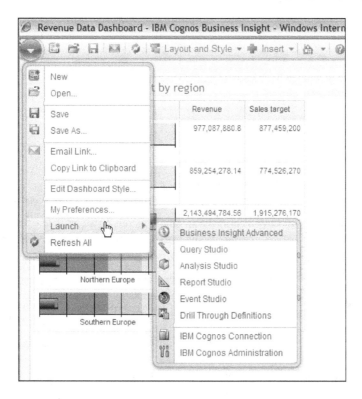

5. Click on **Copy Link to Clipboard**, and paste in a notepad to view the URL.

Dashboard authors can copy the link to clipboard using **Copy Link to Clipboard** and use the URL to navigate from a fancy-looking frontend to the dashboard. Best practice is to design a fancy frontend in HTML/JavaScript and place links to the respective dashboard on the UI. Users can access all the dashboards from a single UI, and need not actually navigate on IBM Cognos Connection.

6. Click on **Edit Dashboard Style...** to open a pop-up window, which allows users to change the look and feel of the dashboard and widgets.

7. Similarly, **My Preferences...** allows users to control product language and content language. It also provides an option to set time zone information. These variables can be used to provide multilingual support. Product language will translate strings shown on the IBM Cognos Business Insight, while content language is used to provide multilingual support while displaying individual widgets.

8. Users can navigate to any other authoring environment, for instance to Report Studio using the **Launch** submenu.

9. All widgets can be refreshed with latest data simultaneously using **Refresh All**.

10. The options given in the following screenshot are also provided as icons on the Toolbar. Tooltips and help texts are provided, to make it convenient for the user:

11. The first icon is **Create new dashboard** followed by icons to open and save the dashboard. The icons for **Email Link** and **Refresh All** are also provided.

12. Now we will see the **Layout and Style** icon, which is to arrange widgets on the canvas and to change the layout of the dashboard. Clicking on **Layout and Style** denoted by the icon opens a submenu with following options:

Menu option	Usability	Icon in submenu
Fit All Widgets to Window	It sizes widgets in such a way so that whole window space on dashboard is occupied by the widgets. No empty space remains on dashboard window.	
Arrange All Widgets to Fit Content	It sizes each widget just to ensure that the whole content is occupied. This may lead to lot of empty space on dashboard.	
Edit Dashboard Style	It allows user to change look and feel of the dashboard and widgets. Background image and colors can be specified along with color scheme for widgets.	

13. The **Insert** icon denoted by opens a submenu to display the **Content** and **Toolbox** tabs on the rightmost Content pane, which we had already discussed in this chapter.

14. The dashboard can be saved as a home page by the user. The icon can be clicked to open a submenu. One of the two choices is **Set Dashboard as Home**, while the other one is **Go to Home Page**. The **Go to Home Page** option allows the user to go to the home page in case some other dashboard is set as the home page for the current user.

15. The dashboard can be added to **Favorites** for a user by clicking on the icon.

16. The **Help** menu denoted by the icon has also been provided for reference to the online documentation.

How it works...

In this recipe we have explored how we can play around with the look and feel of a dashboard as a whole in Cognos Business Insight. We have already set up samples that are shipped with IBM Cognos 10 BI. We used the samples to learn how effectively a user can play around with data on a dashboard.

The next chapter will focus on Cognos Business Insight Advanced UI. We will create some reports and will revisit Cognos Business Insight to use those reports and generate drill-up and drill-down functionality. We will also see how we can deploy and distribute jazzy dashboards, so that it is convenient for business users to access and play around with data.

3
Business Insight Advanced Dashboard

In this chapter we will be:

▶ Opening a dashboard in IBM Cognos Business Insight Advanced

▶ Exploring the **Insertable Objects** pane

▶ Exploring the **Properties** pane

▶ Exploring the Application bar

Introduction

In this chapter we will look at the **graphical user interface** (**GUI**) of Cognos Business Insight Advanced. To reiterate, Cognos Business Insight Advanced is a web-based tool used to author reports and analyze data.

The advanced version enables business users to get an insight into their data without getting into the complexities of the Cognos Report Studio.

The reports created in Cognos Business Insight Advanced can be accessed in Cognos Report Studio as well. Independent reports created using Cognos Business Insight Advanced can be used in Cognos Business Insight to design and develop dashboards.

We will have a look at the interface of Cognos Business Insight Advanced, with which we will create custom reports on different set of data later in this book.

We will then use these reports, in Cognos Business Insight, to design a dashboard.

Opening a dashboard in IBM Cognos Business Insight Advanced

In this recipe we will open an existing dashboard created with Cognos Business Insight Advanced. We will use the GO Sales and Go Data Warehouse samples, which are shipped with IBM Cognos 10 BI setup.

Getting ready

Make sure that IBM Cognos 10 BI Server is up and running. The `GO Sales` and `GO Data Warehouse` samples should also be set up and working.

How to do it...

To open a dashboard in IBM Cognos Business Insight Advanced, perform the following steps:

1. Log on to **IBM Cognos Connection** and navigate to **Public Folders | Samples | Models | GO Data Warehouse (query) | Business Insight Advanced**, as shown in the following screenshot:

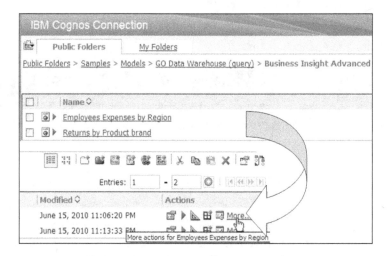

2. Click on the **More...** option, visible on the rightmost side of the **Employees Expenses by Region** report. It will open the **Perform an action – Employees Expenses by Region** window, as shown in the following screenshot:

3. Click on the **Open with Business Insight Advanced** link, as shown in the preceding screenshot. This will open the report in Cognos Business Insight Advanced , as shown in the following screenshot. This is similar to opening a report in Cognos Query Studio where the report actually displays data, unlike in Cognos Report Studio where the report just opens up in the design mode without executing any query, and hence, without any data returned. We will now look at how to open the dashboard in the next step.

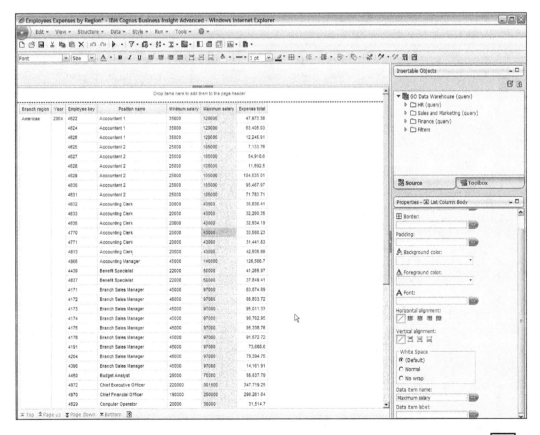

4. Let us go back to **IBM Cognos Connection** and navigate to the folder, as shown in the following screenshot. Click on the **Launch** link, which will open a menu of different authoring environments that a user can choose to create/open a report. Select **Business Insight Advanced**:

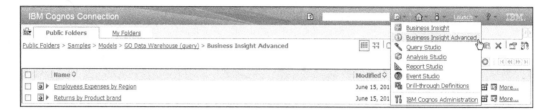

5. Click on the **Open existing** button and navigate to the **Employees Expenses by Region** report to open it in Cognos Business Insight Advanced:

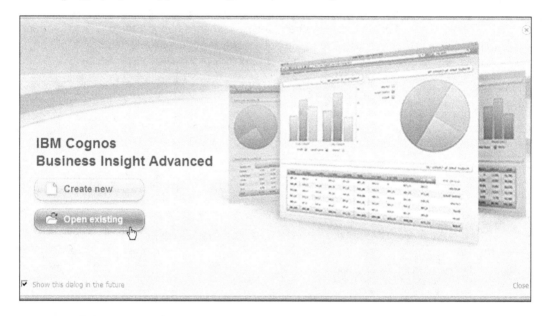

6. This will open the report in Cognos Business Insight, as shown in the following screenshot:

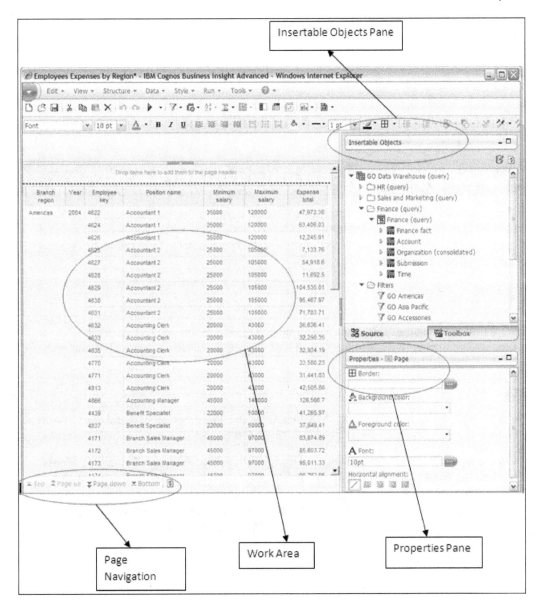

The preceding screenshot displays primary areas of Cognos Business Insight Advanced. We will explore each of these in the following recipes.

How it works...

In this recipe we have used our existing IBM Cognos 10 BI setup and have seen how we can navigate to Cognos Business Insight Advanced. We have seen key areas of its interface.

In the next sections we will focus on each of the components of Cognos Business Insight Advanced in detail. We will discuss what we can do with each of the features provided within the tool.

Exploring the Insertable Objects pane

In this recipe we will explore the **Insertable Objects** pane on Cognos Business Insight Advanced interface. The **Insertable Objects** pane contains objects that can be added to a report by dragging-and-dropping onto the work area. These objects form the basic building blocks of reports and dashboards.

Getting ready

Ensure that IBM Cognos 10 BI Server is running. We will use the `GO Sales` and `GO Data Warehouse` samples that are shipped with IBM Cognos 10 BI setup to complete the recipe.

How to do it...

We will now open an existing report in Cognos Business Insight Advanced and start exploring various features it offers on the interface. Perform the following steps:

1. Log on to Cognos Connection and navigate to **Public Folders | Samples | Models | GO Data Warehouse (query) | Business Insight Advanced**. Open **Employees Expenses by Region** in Cognos Business Insight Advanced, as explained in the previous recipe. Shown on the rightmost side is the **Insertable Objects** pane, which contains objects that can be inserted on to the dashboard:

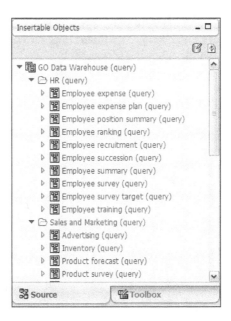

2. As shown in the preceding screenshot, there are two tabs on the interface. The tab on the left-hand side is called **Source** and the one on the right-hand side is called as **Toolbox**.

3. The **Source** tab displays the metadata model, which is the logical representation of the database tables and columns. Users can drag-and-drop these from the metadata model to the work area to create reports and dashboards.

 A report created in Cognos Business Insight Advanced is tightly coupled with a specific metadata model. Each report can further have different objects such as charts, lists, and crosstabs. Cognos Business Insight can be used to design dashboards on top of these reports. Objects from different reports can be added to a single dashboard in Cognos Business Insight, irrespective of the metadata model used to create these reports. Hence, a user is presented with diverse data in the most convenient format, as a single dashboard.

4. For instance, we can expand the metadata model in the **Source** tab. Right-click on **Expense unit quantity** and click on the **Insert** option to drop the query item to the work area, as shown in the following screenshot:

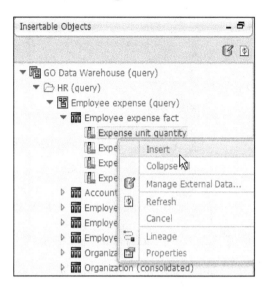

5. The query item can also be inserted in the work area using drag-and-drop, instead of right-clicking on **Insert**.

External data can be imported and used along with enterprise data using the ⬚ icon in the **Insertable Objects** pane. External or personal data from data sources such as Excel, CSV, tab-delimited files, and XML can be imported to supplement enterprise data and used right away by importing external files, defining links between enterprise data and newly imported personal data, and publishing new external data packages. External data packages do not overwrite existing packages but include the existing original package along with new external data. By default, the new package is saved in the **My Folders** area of **IBM Cognos Connection** and appends External Data to the original package name. The user can change the location of where the package is published.

More detailed information regarding external data can be found in the product documentation and is out of the scope of this book.

6. The **Refresh** icon denoted by ⬚ is provided to refresh the contents displayed in the **Insertable Objects** pane. It is useful if the existing metadata model is changed and the author wants to use the latest version of the package.

7. Now we will look at the **Toolbox** tab in the **Insertable Objects** pane in detail. It provides list of objects that are provided by Cognos and can be inserted into the work area. These objects are different from the database objects, and instead, are different widgets provided by Cognos to format and organize data on the dashboard. Refer to the **Toolbox** tab, as shown in the following screenshot:

8. Objects available on the tab can be dragged-and-dropped to the work area. First icon on the tab is **Text Item** denoted by , which allows a user to insert strings on the dashboard for instance titles and subtitles.

9. Similarly, blocks and tables can be inserted on the dashboard using the **Block** and **Table** options respectively, to provide custom formatting.

> Most of the objects available under **Toolbox** should be familiar to users, who already have experience of authoring reports in Cognos Report Studio.

10. **Query Calculation** denoted by 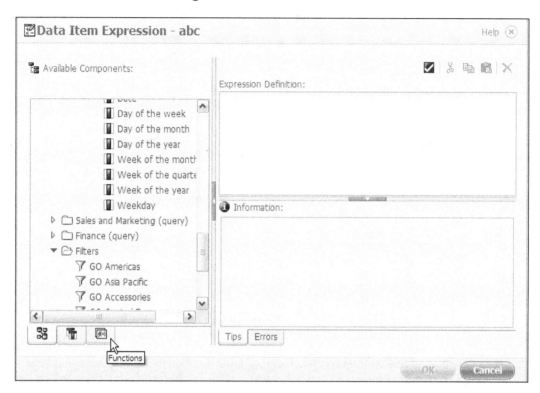 can be added to the dashboard to insert calculations based on existing query items on the dashboard or based on query items in the metadata package. For instance, in the current dashboard, dropping a query calculation would present to the user a dialog to form an expression, as shown in the following screenshot:

11. Note the list of functions available to the users:

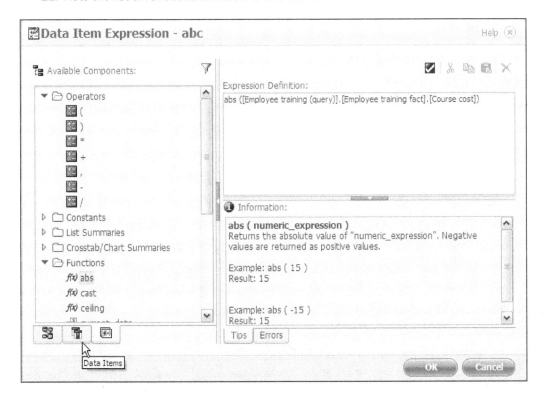

12. There are various options available in the dialog box under different tabs that can be filtered by clicking on the 🔽 icon.

> Hints and tips for using these functions are provided under the **Tips** tab, as shown in the preceding screenshot.

13. An image can be inserted on the dashboard, by clicking on **Image** denoted by the ▦ icon on the **Toolbox** tab. The user needs to browse and specify the location of the image.

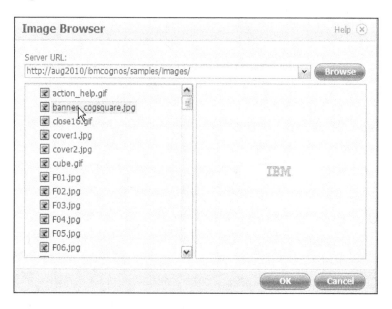

14. The **Crosstab Space** and **Crosstab Space (with fact cells)** options from the **Toolbox** tab can be used to add a crosstab space and a crosstab space with fact cells respectively. Apart from the existing **Crosstab** icon, the **List** option is also provided on the **Toolbox** tab to insert a list. These are the different ways in which data can be shown to the business users:

15. Charts can be added to the dashboard by dragging-and-dropping the **Insert Chart** option denoted by the ▦ icon on the work area. There is a list of charts, which can be used on the dashboard. It is shown in the following screenshot:

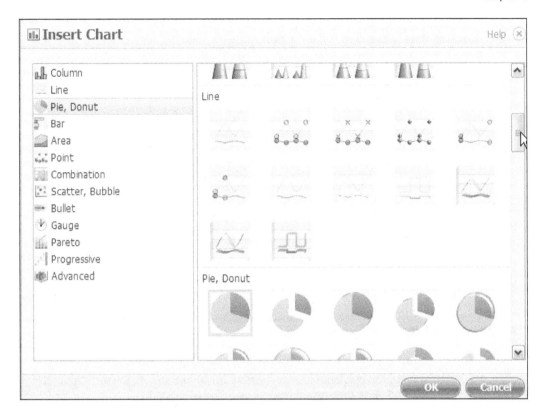

 Tooltips are provided for each of these charts. Help text becomes visible when the user hovers the mouse pointer over these chart icons.

16. Hyperlinks to other web content can be added to the dashboard, by dragging-and-dropping **Hyperlink**, denoted by the ![icon] icon. The URL can be specified as a property of the hyperlink object. This helps in linking the dashboard with other web content, for example, web pages. The user needs to drop the hyperlink object onto the work area, right-click on the object, and click on **Edit URL...** to specify the URL, as shown in the following screenshot:

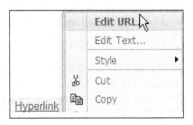

17. Constants such as date, time, and page number can also be added to the dashboard using the **Date**, **Time**, and **Page Number** icons respectively. Icons for each of these are provided on the **Toolbox** tab, as shown in the following screenshot:

How it works...

In this recipe we have seen various insertable objects available on the Cognos Business Insight Advanced interface. We have seen them in the context of the GO Sales and GO Data Warehouse samples, which we had already set up. The following table lists the features and uses of the **Insertable Objects** pane:

Feature	Use
Source tab	This contains the database objects represented in the form of logical model called metadata package. As a thumb rule, here, a table is called as a query subject and a column as a query item. These can be dragged-and-dropped to the work area to bring actual data on to the dashboard.
Toolbox tab	This provides list of objects provided by Cognos, which are used to represent the data from the **Source** tab in the required format. This further modifies look and feel of the objects and the way users can view data on the dashboard.

Now we will focus on other areas of the Cognos Business Insight Advanced interface. In the next chapters we will create our own custom dashboards. We will see how we can place different objects from different dashboards and arrive at a single view of data using IBM Cognos Business Insight.

Exploring the Properties pane

In this recipe we will explore the **Properties** pane on the Cognos Business Insight Advanced interface. Each widget we drag-and-drop onto the work area has a list of properties that can be set to customize its look and feel as well as behavior.

The **Properties** pane displays the properties for each widget we use to design the dashboard. For instance, a bar chart is a widget, which we might want to place on the dashboard. It has its own set of properties such as color palette and size, which can be adjusted, to customize its look and feel.

Getting ready

Ensure IBM Cognos 10 BI Server is started. The GO Sales and GO Data Warehouse samples should be configured on the server and working.

How to do it...

We will now open a sample report in Cognos Business Insight and explore the **Properties** pane in detail. Perform the following steps:

1. Log on to the Cognos Connection and navigate to **Public Folders | Samples | Models | Interactive Samples**. Open **Recruitment Report** in Cognos Business Insight Advanced, as shown in the following screenshot:

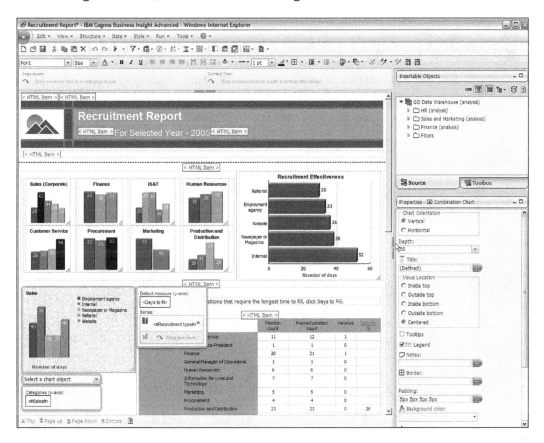

2. The report shown in the preceding screenshot has been created using Cognos Report Studio. We have opened this report in Cognos Business Insight Advanced by clicking on **More... | Open with Business Insight Advanced**, as we have seen in the *Opening a dashboard in IBM Cognos Business Insight Advanced* recipe.

3. Now we will explore the **Properties** pane at the bottom-right corner for different objects on the work area.

4. As shown in the following screenshot, select the **Recruitment Effectiveness** column bar chart, which will lead to the corresponding chart properties being displayed in the **Properties** pane, as shown in the following screenshot:

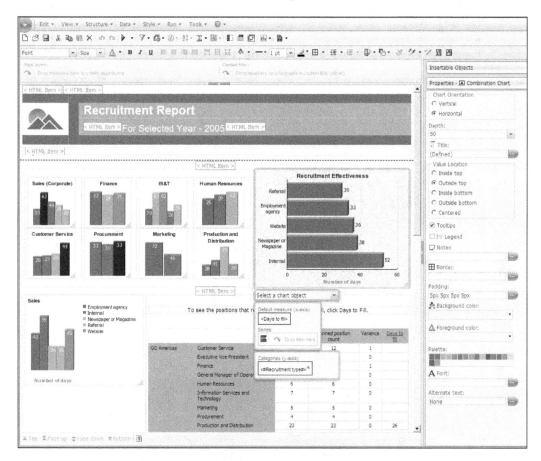

5. As we can see in the preceding screenshot, there are different properties visible in **Properties – Combination Chart**. Let us change a few of these to see how the view of work area changes in accordance to the **Properties** pane.

6. Let us change the **Chart Orientation** from **Horizontal** to **Vertical**, as shown in the following screenshot:

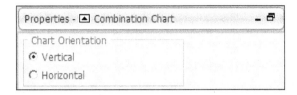

7. This will change the layout of the corresponding chart—**Recruitment Effectiveness** from **Vertical** to **Horizontal**, as shown in the following screenshot:

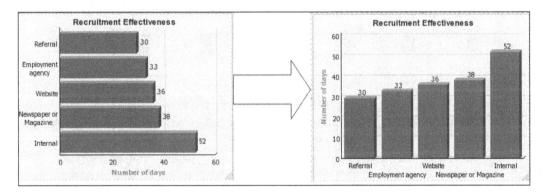

 Different settings in the **Properties** pane are autoselected. This would imply that a property setting, when changed, causes the corresponding change on the work area on the fly. The user doesn't have to execute the report to view the effects of changed settings.

8. Now we will see another important setting—**Value Location**, as shown in the following screenshot:

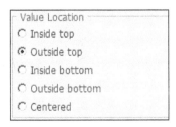

9. The **Value Location** setting controls where the actual data values are displayed on the chart. For instance, in the current setting, values are displayed outside the bar, as we have selected the **Outside top** option. Let us change this setting to **Inside top** to display the values inside the bar, which should change the view, as shown in the following screenshot:

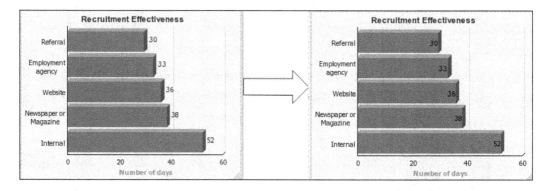

10. Another important property is to hide/show tooltips, which can be adjusted by clearing/checking the ☑ Tooltips icon. The **Tooltips** option, when enabled, will display values and other help text on the chart, or on mouse hover actions.

11. Similarly, other cosmetic features such as title, chart palette, font, background color, foreground color can be adjusted to customize the look and feel of the chart object on the dashboard.

12. Now we will click on **Crosstab** and see its properties in the right-hand side pane:

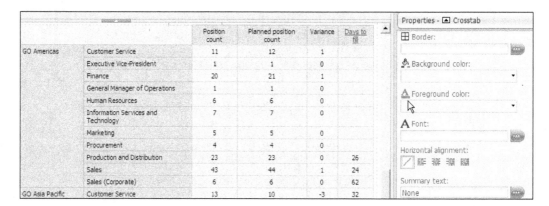

13. Note that properties for a crosstab are different than that of a chart. We can adjust basic look and feel of the crosstab in terms of **Border**, **Background color**, **Foreground color**, **Font**, and so on.

 Take a note of the ⬚ icon, on the **Properties** title bar, which can be clicked to view the hierarchy in which the current object falls. A higher-level object can also be selected using this.

How it works...

In this recipe we have seen how we can configure the setting of each object/widget on the dashboard independently. We saw how changing a few properties for a chart alters its look and feel on the work area. Similar options exist for other objects such as table, textbox, and list. Properties also vary across different type of charts.

The next recipes in this chapter will focus on other areas of Cognos Business Insight Advanced and how they can be used to create and customize dashboards.

Exploring the Application bar – general options

In this recipe we will explore another important area of Cognos Business Insight Advanced. We have seen similar explanations in previous chapter as well, in the context of Cognos Business Insight. In this recipe we will revisit and look at the kind of capabilities it provides on the Cognos Business Insight Advanced interface.

We will divide the Application bar into two areas for the sake of simplicity. First part will focus on the generic options that most word processors have. The second part will cover what is specific to Cognos Business Insight Advanced.

Getting ready

Make sure that IBM Cognos 10 BI server is up along with the GO Sales and GO Data Warehouse samples.

How to do it...

We will now open a report in Cognos Business Insight Advanced and look at the Application bar in detail. Perform the following steps:

1. Log on to Cognos Connection and navigate to **Public Folders | Samples | Models | Interactive Samples**. Open **Recruitment Report** in Cognos Business Insight Advanced. We will focus on the Application bar in this recipe. It is circled in red in the following screenshot:

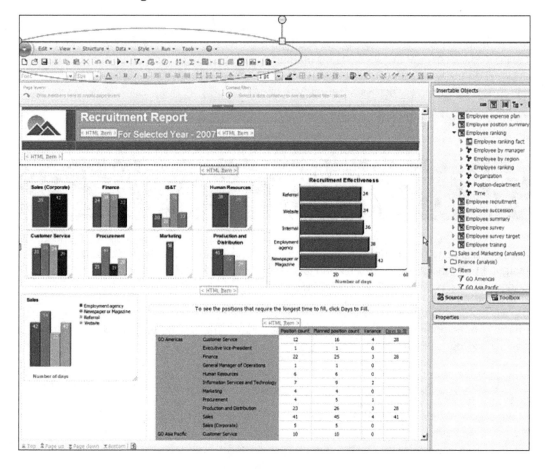

We have already visited most of this part of the Application bar while discussing Cognos Business Insight. In this recipe, we will primarily focus on its most important additional features.

2. The Application bar is provided with various options to manage the dashboard as a whole. For instance, options have been provided to create a new dashboard, open an existing dashboard, and save a dashboard. The first three icons are dedicated to this functionality.

[Do not forget to use mouse hover tooltips to get a quick hint regarding the icons on the Application bar.]

3. Next are the **Cut**, **Copy**, **Paste**, and **Delete** icons denoted by ✂ ▤ ▦ ✕ respectively, which are used to cut, copy, paste, and delete the objects on the dashboard. The **Undo** and **Redo** functionalities are also provided upon clicking ↺ ↻.

4. Keep the report open as it is now, and proceed to the next recipe.

How it works...

In this recipe we have seen the general options on the Application toolbar, which are pretty common and can be found in any modern word-processing software.

In the next recipe we will focus on Cognos-specific options present on the Application bar.

Exploring the Application bar – Cognos-specific options

In this recipe we will learn more about the Application bar in terms of Cognos-specific options. We will proceed directly from where we left off in the previous recipe.

How to do it...

We will focus on the Application bar, circled in red, as shown in the previous recipe. It is assumed that we already have **Recruitment Report** at the location—**Public Folders** | **Samples** | **Models** | **Interactive Samples** opened in front of us, in Cognos Business Insight Advanced tool. To explore the Cognos-specific options of the Application bar, perform the following steps:

1. We can execute a dashboard in various formats by clicking on the ▶⋅ icon:

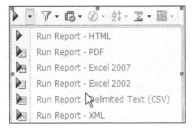

2. Data on the dashboard can be filtered using one of the options provided under the icon. The user needs to select an object on the dashboard and click on the **Filter** icon to apply a filter in different possible ways, as shown in the following screenshot.

> Filters are used to limit the amount of data appearing on the dashboard, which in turn improves readability and performance. It helps to focus on just the dataset in which the user is interested.

3. For instance, let us apply a filter on the **Recruitment Effectiveness** column bar chart, by clicking on it and then on the **Filter** icon:

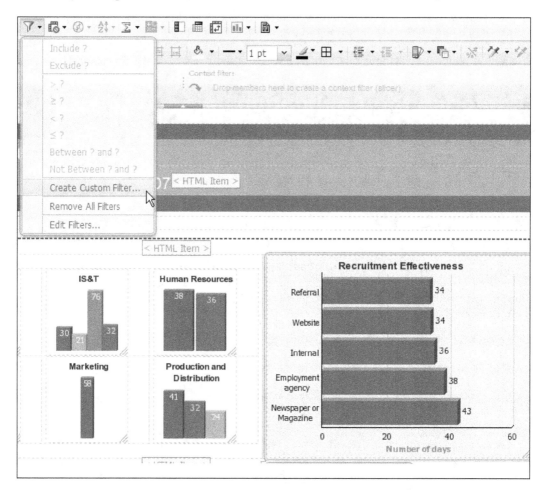

4. As shown in preceding screenshot, some options in the drop-down menu are disabled, as they are not relevant with respect to the **Recruitment Effectiveness** column bar chart. We will click on **Create Custom Filter...** to apply the filter to the chart.

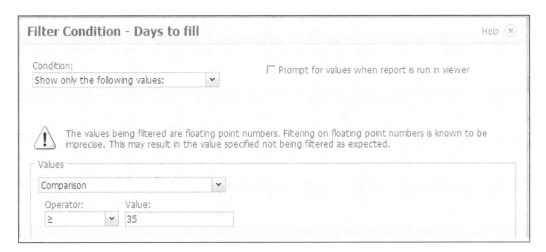

5. In the preceding screenshot we want to apply a filter that should only allow values greater than or equal to 35. In the **Filter Condition – Days to fill** dialog box, click on the **OK** button to apply the filter. The chart gets filtered, as shown in the following screenshot:

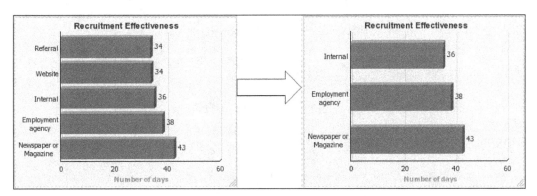

6. The same drop-down menu under the **Filter** icon can be used to edit filters by clicking on **Edit Filters...** and also to remove filters. A user just needs to ensure that the correct object on the dashboard is selected:

7. Click on **Remove All Filters** to reset the chart as before. Now we will apply a different text-based filter on the crosstab column, as shown in the following screenshot:

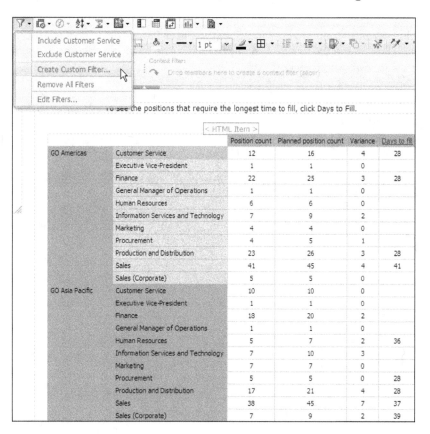

		Position count	Planned position count	Variance	Days to fill
GO Americas	Customer Service	12	16	4	28
	Executive Vice-President	1	1	0	
	Finance	22	25	3	28
	General Manager of Operations	1	1	0	
	Human Resources	6	6	0	
	Information Services and Technology	7	9	2	
	Marketing	4	4	0	
	Procurement	4	5	1	
	Production and Distribution	23	26	3	28
	Sales	41	45	4	41
	Sales (Corporate)	5	5	0	
GO Asia Pacific	Customer Service	10	10	0	
	Executive Vice-President	1	1	0	
	Finance	18	20	2	
	General Manager of Operations	1	1	0	
	Human Resources	5	7	2	36
	Information Services and Technology	7	10	3	
	Marketing	7	7	0	
	Procurement	5	5	0	28
	Production and Distribution	17	21	4	28
	Sales	38	45	7	37
	Sales (Corporate)	7	9	2	39

8. It will open a new dialog box, which we can use to create a filter condition. Note that this time the **Filter Condition** dialog box is different than what we had in the case of the chart, where we were applying a filter on numeric values.

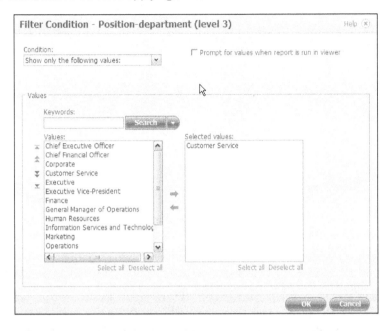

9. Here we want the crosstab to show data only for **Finance**, **Marketing**, **Operations**, **Sales**, and **Procurement**. We will use 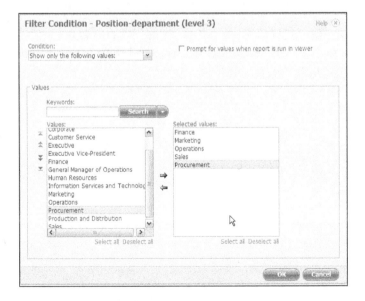 to select and deselect values and apply the filter, as shown in the following screenshot:

10. This should modify the crosstab, as shown in the following screenshot:

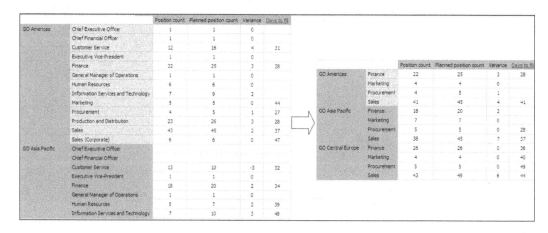

11. Again, the filters can be removed and edited using the same drop-down menu under the **Filter** icon from the Application bar.

12. More than one filter can be combined to further refine the data appearing on the dashboard. The user just needs to know which type of filter should be applied to which part of the object. Use ⬆ on the **Properties** pane title bar to select relevant object.

13. Now remove all the filters we have applied so far. Close the dashboard and navigate to the **Public Folders | Samples | Models | GO Data Warehouse (query) | Business Insight Advanced** directory.

14. Open the **Returns by Product brand** report in IBM Cognos Business Insight Advanced.

15. The following screenshot displays a list on the dashboard showing the **Returns by Product brand** report. We have many products in this report for which we do not have **Return quantity**. If we wish to hide these rows from the current dashboard view, the **Suppress** functionality denoted by 🔯, which is available on the Application bar, can be used.

Returns by Product brand

Product line	Promotion code	Product brand	Return quantity	Reason description
Camping Equipment	0	Canyon Mule	3,331	Defective product
Camping Equipment	10212	Canyon Mule	2,537	Incomplete product
Camping Equipment	10213	Canyon Mule	5,204	Unsatisfactory product
Camping Equipment	10228	Canyon Mule	8,324	Wrong product ordered
Camping Equipment	50125	Canyon Mule	4,610	Wrong product shipped
Camping Equipment	60506	Canyon Mule		
Camping Equipment	60535	Canyon Mule		
Camping Equipment	60607	Canyon Mule		
Camping Equipment	60614	Canyon Mule		
Camping Equipment	60616	Canyon Mule		
Camping Equipment	60722	Canyon Mule		
Camping Equipment	60724	Canyon Mule		
Camping Equipment	60728	Canyon Mule		
Camping Equipment	90109	Canyon Mule		
Camping Equipment	0	EverGlow	1,892	Defective product
Camping Equipment	10209	EverGlow	23,333	Incomplete product
Camping Equipment	10210	EverGlow	3,855	Unsatisfactory product
Camping Equipment	10211	EverGlow	6,172	Wrong product ordered
Camping Equipment	10227	EverGlow	4,334	Wrong product shipped
Camping Equipment	50107	EverGlow		

16. On the work Area, select the list and click on the **Suppress** icon on the Application bar to open the menu, as shown in the following screenshot:

17. Click on **Suppression Options...** to learn more about this feature. Suppression refers to not showing those rows or columns or both, for which the selected widget has one or more of the conditions (stated in the right-hand side pane of the following screenshot) satisfied. By default, **None** is selected, and hence, no suppression is applied to the list. Let us select the list and configure **Suppression Options** to hide rows having zero values or missing values by selecting **Zero values** and **Missing values** under the **Suppress the following** section, as shown in the following screenshot:

18. Click on the **OK** button to see the difference, as shown in the following screenshot. Clearly, the rows having missing values have been hidden or suppressed:

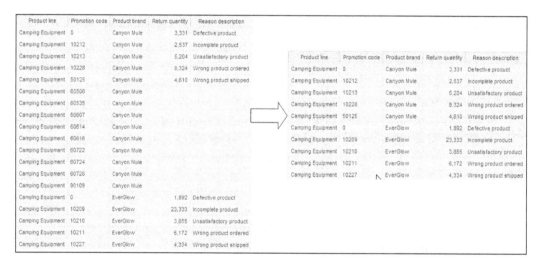

 While applying any of the controls from the Application bar, do not forget to select the proper widget using the ⬆ icon on the **Properties** pane.

19. As explained earlier, the user can click on the ▲ icon and select any object that falls in the current hierarchy. For instance, in the preceding example we already have selected **List**, and hence, selecting the ▲ icon on the **Properties** pane will show objects higher in the hierarchy. Hence, a user can select **Page Body** from the **Properties** pane of **List**, as shown in the following screenshot:

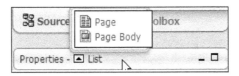

20. If you have already applied suppression, it can be removed by selecting **None** under the **Suppression** section of the **Suppression Options** window. Similarly suppression can be applied to a crosstab, where **Suppression Options** allow a user to hide rows, columns, or both.

21. Close the dashboard without saving it. Navigate to **Public Folders** | **Samples** | **Models** | **Interactive Samples**. Open **Top 10 Retailers for 2005** in IBM Cognos Business Insight Advanced, as shown in the following screenshot:

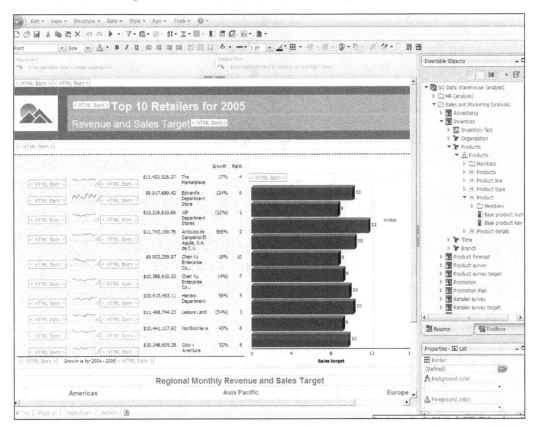

22. The next options that might interest us are drill up and drill down, which can be selected by clicking on the ⬚ icon. This needs the dashboard to use a **dimensionally modeled relational** (**DMR**) package, which is currently not the case. We will revisit the drill functionality, and hence, the icon later.

23. The user can perform layout sorting by clicking on the ⬚ icon. Select **List Column Body** and click on ⬚, as shown in the following screenshot:

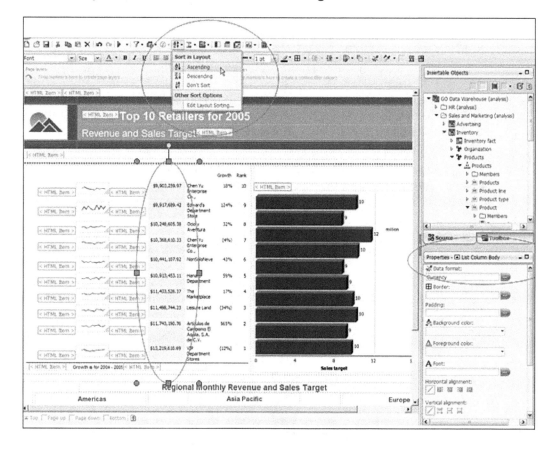

24. It provides the options such as **Ascending** and **Descending** to sort items in ascending or descending order. Click on **Edit Layout Sorting...** to learn more.

25. We have dragged-and-dropped **Revenue,2005** to the **Detail Sort List** option under **Groups**, as shown in the preceding screenshot. Note that we have already selected **List Column Body** displaying **Revenue,2005** highlighted in the background. Click on the **OK** button.

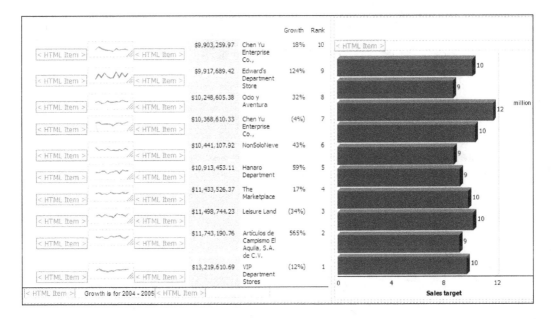

26. Note that now the list is sorted in the ascending order of **Revenue,2005**.

27. We can also summarize data on the report by clicking on ⬛ in the appropriate manner.

28. Let us insert a total summary in the **Revenue,2005** column on the dashboard. We will be selecting **List Column Body** for the **Revenue,2005** column, as highlighted in the following screenshot. Click on the ⬛ icon to open a menu of summary functions:

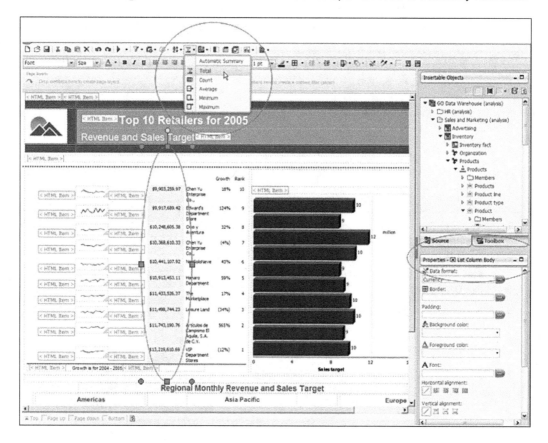

29. Note that a new row displaying a summary has been added at the bottom, as shown in the following screenshot in bold:

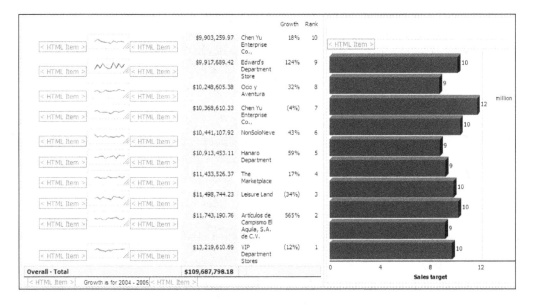

30. Calculations can also be added to the dashboard based on the object selected. The user needs to select an appropriate object and click on <image id="icon" /> to open a menu. Menu shows the operations that can be performed on the object.

31. Let us select another column—**Retailer** and try to insert a calculation based on that. Note that the **Retailer** column is next to **Revenue,2005**, as highlighted in the following screenshot. Click on <image id="icon" /> to open the menu. The menu shows the list of operations that can be performed on the column. We want another column to display the first 10 characters from values shown in the **Retailer** column.

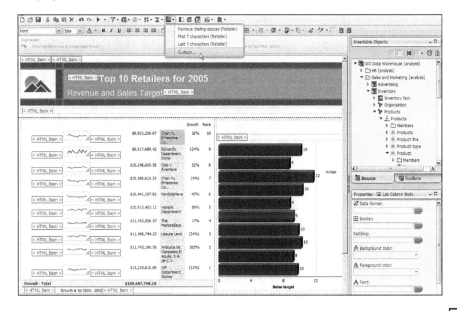

32. Click on the **Custom...** option to open the **Insert Custom Calculation** dialog box. Select **First Characters** from the **Operation** drop-down menu and enter **10** in the **Number** textbox. Define a name for the new data item under the **New data item name** section as **Retailer Short Name**, as shown in the following screenshot:

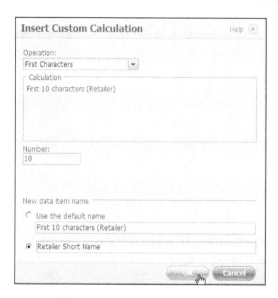

33. Click on the **OK** button to view the newly inserted calculated column.

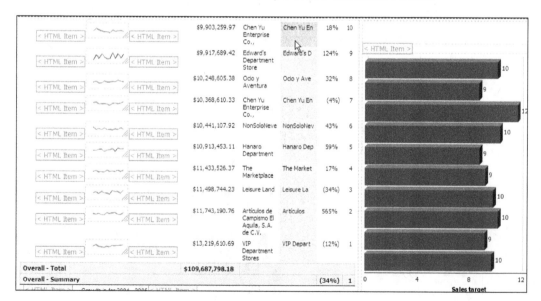

34. Similarly, when we click on a numerical column, operations that can be performed are different. For instance, select the **Revenue,2005** column and click on the ![icon] icon. It will show different sets of operations that can be performed on the column.

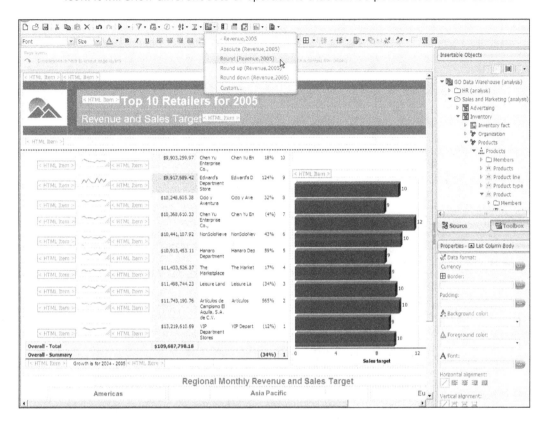

35. Close the dashboard without saving anything. Navigate to **Public Folders** | **Samples** | **Models** | **GO Data Warehouse (query)** | **Business Insight Advanced** and open **Returns by Product brand** in IBM Cognos Business Insight Advanced.

36. The dashboard has a list of products, which were returned due to one of the reasons specified in the **Reason description** column, as shown in the following screenshot:

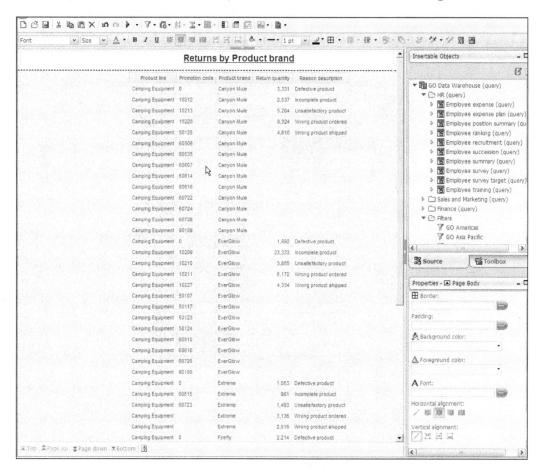

37. Let us see how we can make the report more readable using some options in the Application bar. Let us first reorganize the columns on the dashboard by dragging-and-dropping them on the work area, as shown in the following screenshot:

Product line	Product brand	Reason description	Promotion code	Return quantity
Camping Equipment	Canyon Mule	Defective product	0	3,331
Camping Equipment	Canyon Mule	Incomplete product	10212	2,537
Camping Equipment	Canyon Mule	Unsatisfactory product	10213	5,204
Camping Equipment	Canyon Mule	Wrong product ordered	10228	8,324
Camping Equipment	Canyon Mule	Wrong product shipped	50125	4,610
Camping Equipment	Canyon Mule		60506	
Camping Equipment	Canyon Mule		60535	
Camping Equipment	Canyon Mule		60607	
Camping Equipment	Canyon Mule		60614	
Camping Equipment	Canyon Mule		60616	
Camping Equipment	Canyon Mule		60722	
Camping Equipment	Canyon Mule		60724	
Camping Equipment	Canyon Mule		60728	
Camping Equipment	Canyon Mule		90109	
Camping Equipment	EverGlow	Defective product	0	1,892
Camping Equipment	EverGlow	Incomplete product	10209	23,333
Camping Equipment	EverGlow	Unsatisfactory product	10210	3,855
Camping Equipment	EverGlow	Wrong product ordered	10211	6,172
Camping Equipment	EverGlow	Wrong product shipped	10227	4,334

38. On the Application bar, there is a ▦ icon, which can be used to group/ungroup the selected data in the list. Click on the **Product line** column and click on the ▦ icon to group the list in the **Product line** column, as shown in the following screenshot:

Product line	Product brand	Reason description	Promotion code	Return quantity
Camping Equipment	Canyon Mule	Defective product	0	3,331
	Canyon Mule	Incomplete product	10212	2,537
	Canyon Mule	Unsatisfactory product	10213	5,204
	Canyon Mule	Wrong product ordered	10228	8,324
	Canyon Mule	Wrong product shipped	50125	4,610
	Canyon Mule		60506	
	Canyon Mule		60535	
	Canyon Mule		60607	
	Canyon Mule		60614	
	Canyon Mule		60616	
	Canyon Mule		60722	
	Canyon Mule		60724	
	Canyon Mule		60728	
	Canyon Mule		90109	
	EverGlow	Defective product	0	1,892
	EverGlow	Incomplete product	10209	23,333
	EverGlow	Unsatisfactory product	10210	3,855
	EverGlow	Wrong product ordered	10211	6,172
	EverGlow	Wrong product shipped	10227	4,334

39. Similarly, group the **Product brand** and **Reason description** columns in order:

Product line	Product brand	Reason description	Promotion code	Return quantity
Camping Equipment	Canyon Mule	Defective product	0	3,331
		Defective product - Summary		**3,331**
		Incomplete product	10212	2,537
		Incomplete product - Summary		**2,537**
		Unsatisfactory product	10213	5,204
		Unsatisfactory product - Summary		**5,204**
		Wrong product ordered	10228	8,324
		Wrong product ordered - Summary		**8,324**
		Wrong product shipped	50125	4,610
		Wrong product shipped - Summary		**4,610**
			60506	
			60535	
			60607	
			60614	
			60616	
			60722	
			60724	
			60728	
			90109	
		- Summary		
	Canyon Mule - Summary			**24,006**

40. As seen in the preceding screenshot, data is grouped accordingly and summary footers have been added for each data group in hierarchical order. Let us delete the **Promotion code** column from the list by selecting the column and clicking on ⊠ on the Application bar. This shows an aggregated view of the data, where the total return quantity is shown in the **Return quantity** column for each **Reason description**, **Product brand**, and **Product line** in order:

Product line	Product brand	Reason description	Return quantity
Camping Equipment	Canyon Mule	Defective product	3,331
		Incomplete product	2,537
		Unsatisfactory product	5,204
		Wrong product ordered	8,324
		Wrong product shipped	4,610
	Canyon Mule - Summary		**24,006**
	EverGlow	Defective product	1,892
		Incomplete product	23,333
		Unsatisfactory product	3,855
		Wrong product ordered	6,172
		Wrong product shipped	4,334
	EverGlow - Summary		**39,586**
	Extreme	Defective product	1,053
		Incomplete product	981
		Unsatisfactory product	1,493
		Wrong product ordered	3,136
		Wrong product shipped	2,016
	Extreme - Summary		**8,679**
	Firefly	Defective product	2,214
		Incomplete product	4,281
		Unsatisfactory product	3,964
		Wrong product ordered	5,581
		Wrong product shipped	7,930
	Firefly - Summary		**23,970**

41. Now we want to convert the list into a crosstab view. We have a ⊞ icon to do that. We just need to select a column, **Reason description** in our case, and click on ⊞. The column we have selected will become a column of the crosstab and other non-numerical columns will become rows. Numerical measures will be displayed at crosstab intersection, as shown in the following screenshot:

42. This will change the list view to the crosstab view, as shown in the following screenshot:

Returns by Product brand

Return quantity		Defective product	Incomplete product	Unsatisfactory product	Wrong product ordered	Wrong product shipped	Summary
Personal Accessories	Alpha	8,128	1,077	2,903	8,889	12,830	33,827
	Antoni	4,019	1,120	1,495	6,173	8,182	20,989
	Edge	6,618	12,809	9,125	11,763	10,501	50,816
	Epoch	4,109	708	2,840	6,763	9,299	23,719
	Extreme	758	732	732	2,286	2,321	6,829
	Glacier	963	2,490	3,735	3,902	4,043	15,133
	Mountain Man	653	1,225	1,527	1,815	2,416	7,636
	Polar	1,192	1,504	1,533	2,160	1,232	7,621
	Relax	9,690	1,804	3,533	18,274	23,400	56,701
	Seeker	869	1,169	1,382	1,985	1,354	6,759
	Trakker	8,165	1,922	5,375	14,020	21,471	50,953
	Xray	1,126	248	754	1,963	1,826	5,917
	Summary	**46,290**	**26,808**	**34,934**	**79,993**	**98,875**	**286,900**
Golf Equipment	Blue Steel	126	2,082	568	1,694	1,369	5,839
	Course Pro	5,017	2,234	8,471	14,304	10,192	40,218
	Hailstorm	1,078	1,501	1,029	2,038	1,544	7,190
	Summary	**6,221**	**5,817**	**10,068**	**18,036**	**13,105**	**53,247**
Outdoor Protection	BugShield	27,272		86,485	2,363	940	117,060
	Extreme	21,835		41,969	5,845	2,610	72,255
	Relief	1,861	374	4,988	660	193	8,076
	Sun	28,383		97,043	3,284	3,467	132,177
	Summary	**79,351**	**374**	**230,481**	**12,152**	**7,210**	**329,568**
Camping Equipment	Canyon Mule	3,331	2,537	5,204	8,324	4,610	24,006
	EverGlow	1,892	23,333	3,855	6,172	4,334	39,586
	Extreme	1,053	981	1,493	3,136	2,016	8,679
	Firefly	2,214	4,281	3,964	5,581	7,930	23,970
	Hibernator	6,836	4,355	5,985	6,587	3,202	26,965
	Star	1,706	3,540	8,822	16,678	8,760	39,506
	TrailChef	19,014	18,016	32,226	51,128	21,347	141,731
	Summary	**36,046**	**57,043**	**61,549**	**97,606**	**52,199**	**304,443**

43. Clearly, the report has now become more readable with summary sections added to the data.

44. Rows and columns in the crosstab can be swapped by clicking on the ⊡ icon on the Application bar. It will just change the crosstab view by replacing current columns with what we have in rows and vice versa. Let us click on the icon and see the results, as shown in the following screenshot:

Return quantity	Personal Accessories													Golf Equipment			
	Alpha	Antoni	Edge	Epoch	Extreme	Glacier	Mountain Man	Polar	Relax	Seeker	Trakker	Xray	Summary	Blue Steel	Course Pro	Hailstorm	Summary
Defective product	8,128	4,019	6,618	4,109	758	963	653	1,192	9,690	869	8,165	1,126	46,290	126	5,017	1,078	6,221
Incomplete product	1,077	1,120	12,809	708	732	2,490	1,225	1,504	1,804	1,169	1,922	248	26,808	2,082	2,234	1,501	5,817
Unsatisfactory product	2,903	1,495	9,125	2,840	732	3,735	1,527	1,533	3,533	1,382	5,375	754	34,934	568	8,471	1,029	10,068
Wrong product ordered	8,889	6,173	11,763	6,763	2,286	3,902	1,815	2,160	18,274	1,985	14,020	1,963	79,993	1,894	14,304	2,038	18,036
Wrong product shipped	12,830	8,182	10,501	9,299	2,321	4,043	2,416	1,232	23,400	1,354	21,471	1,826	98,875	1,369	10,192	1,544	13,105
Summary	33,827	20,989	50,816	23,719	6,829	15,133	7,636	7,621	56,701	6,759	50,953	5,917	286,900	5,839	40,218	7,190	53,247

45. Let us remove the **Product brand** level from the column and arrive at the layout as shown in the following screenshot. We are only interested in knowing how much quantity is returned for every **Product line**, **Reason description** combination.

Returns by Product brand						
Return quantity	Camping Equipment	Golf Equipment	Mountaineering Equipment	Outdoor Protection	Personal Accessories	Summary
Defective product	36,046	6,221	15,492	79,351	46,290	183,400
Incomplete product	57,043	5,817	8,176	374	26,808	98,218
Unsatisfactory product	61,549	10,068	27,012	230,481	34,934	364,044
Wrong product ordered	97,606	18,036	24,688	12,152	79,993	232,475
Wrong product shipped	52,199	13,105	30,765	7,210	98,875	202,154
Summary	304,443	53,247	106,133	329,568	286,900	1,080,291

46. Now let us click on the **Insert Chart** icon denoted by 📊▾ to insert a chart representation of the crosstab on the dashboard. Clicking on the **Insert Chart** icon will open a menu, displaying a list of charts that can be used to render the results, as shown in the following screenshot:

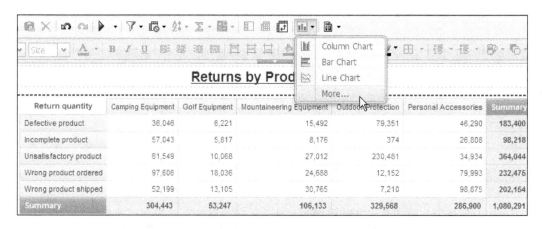

47. Clicking on the **More...** option will open a complete menu of charts along with description as help text, in a menu. Select the **Pie, Donut** chart and click on the **OK** button, as shown in the following screenshot:

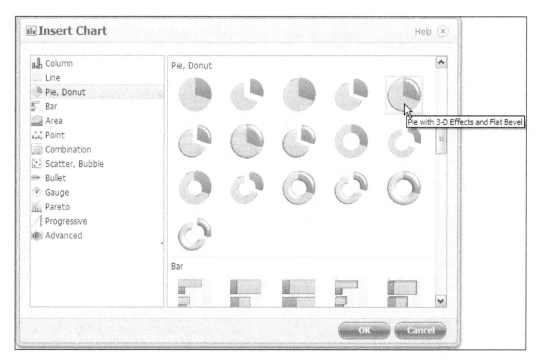

48. This will insert a pie chart on the dashboard, which represents data on the crosstab:

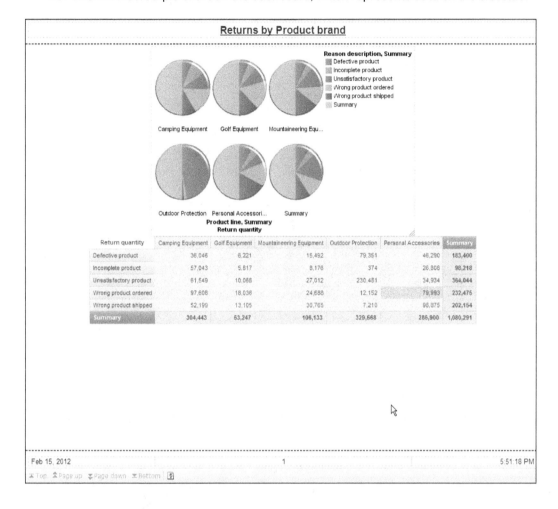

Return quantity	Camping Equipment	Golf Equipment	Mountaineering Equipment	Outdoor Protection	Personal Accessories	Summary
Defective product	36,046	6,221	15,492	79,351	46,290	183,400
Incomplete product	57,043	5,817	8,176	374	26,808	98,218
Unsatisfactory product	61,549	10,068	27,012	230,481	34,934	364,044
Wrong product ordered	97,606	18,036	24,688	12,152	79,993	232,476
Wrong product shipped	52,199	13,105	30,765	7,210	98,875	202,154
Summary	304,443	53,247	106,133	329,568	286,900	1,080,291

Top   Page up   Page down   Bottom

49. The page layout can now be changed to make it visually more appealing by clicking on the ⬚ icon on the Application bar. Let us select one of the layout options, as shown in the following screenshot:

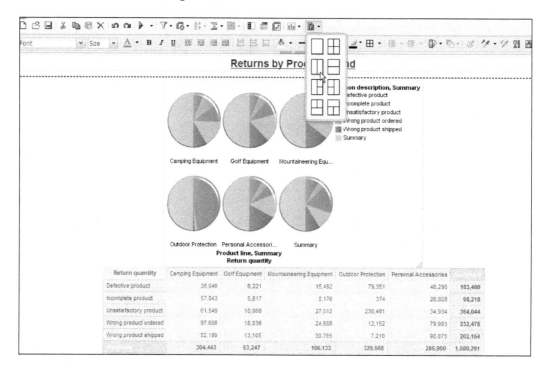

50. This will organize the current content on the dashboard in one of the predefined page templates making our dashboard readable, informative, and visually appealing.

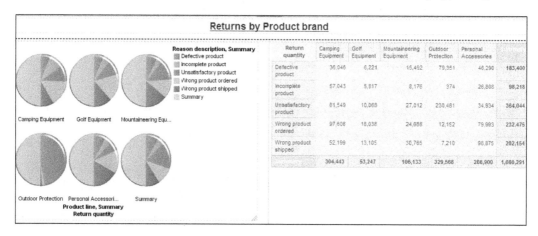

51. There are options available to change style, color scheme, font, background color, border layout, and alignments of various objects on the dashboard. These options are simple and intuitive to understand and should be used to make the dashboard more appealing to the eyes:

52. Note that help texts are provided on mouse hover on all the icons present on the UI.

53. Similarly, we can add more content to the dashboard and organize it to create user intuitive dashboards. Close all the windows without saving anything.

The user can also at any point in time, click on any of the widgets, right-click, and choose from a set of options in a menu. These options are same as what we saw on the Application bar. We just have different ways to navigate and apply these options for different widgets.

How it works...

We have seen how to create a dashboard using the options on the Application bar. The options provide the user with the flexibility that he/she needs to view different aspects of data in a user-intuitive and visually appealing format.

Later chapters will focus on the drill-up and drill-down functionality and how a user can create dashboards from scratch. We will see how we can assemble widgets created in different studios and with different data to arrive at a single view, which can be delivered to users in desired ways, so that effective decisions can be taken in time.

4
Creating Dashboards in IBM Cognos Business Insight Advanced

In this chapter we will be:

- ▶ Creating your first dashboard – defining basic layout
- ▶ Inserting a chart widget
- ▶ Inserting a crosstab widget
- ▶ Formatting and arriving at the final layout
- ▶ Performing drill up and drill down
- ▶ Applying conditional formatting to the dashboard

Introduction

In this chapter we will create our first dashboard using Cognos Business Insight Advanced. We will use the sample **GO Sales (analysis)** package shipped with IBM Cognos 10 BI setup. We will use and explore the most important features that Cognos Business Insight Advanced offers while creating the dashboard.

Creating your first dashboard – defining basic layout

We will start by creating our first dashboard using Cognos Business Insight. We will save the dashboard and use its individual components in later chapters, to assemble enterprise-level dashboards using Cognos Business Insight.

 An enterprise-level dashboard can display data from different sources. A report/dashboard created in Report Studio or Business Insight Advanced can be one of them. Business Insight can be used to design such enterprise-level dashboards by picking, for instance, a bar chart from report A, a crosstab from dashboard B, and a pie chart from report C. Graphical user interface provides flexibility to pick widgets from each of these reports selectively.

Getting ready

Make sure that IBM Cognos 10 BI Service is started and IBM Cognos Samples are installed. Log on to Cognos Connection.

How to do it...

To create a dashboard, perform the following steps:

1. Let us now use the **GO Sales (analysis)** package installed with samples and create our first dashboard. In this recipe we will define its basic layout. In subsequent recipes we will add more components to it.

2. Navigate to **Public Folders | GO Sales (analysis)**. Click on **Business Insight Advanced** from the **Launch** menu, as shown in the following screenshot. It will open the metadata package in Cognos Business Insight Advanced.

3. Click on the **Create new** button as we want to create a new dashboard:

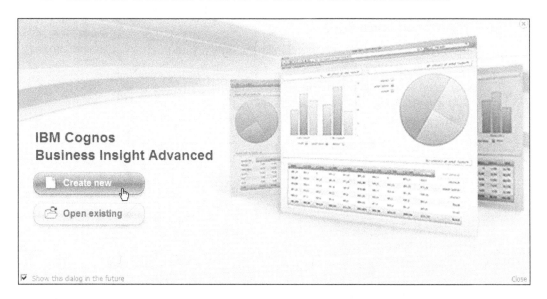

4. Click on the **Blank** icon to start with a blank dashboard. Click on the **OK** button to continue, as shown in the following screenshot:

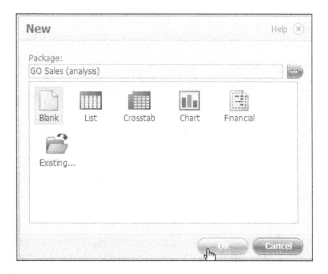

5. Click on **List**, **Crosstab**, **Chart**, or **Financial** if you want to create a particular type of dashboard, which matches one of these in the layout. For instance, the **List** icon should be selected from the **New** dialog box to create a tabular-styled dashboard. This will open Cognos Business Insight Advanced, with a **List** object inserted by default.

6. Custom templates can also be defined, which when applied while creating reports and dashboards from the existing folder, will ensure that a common look and feel is applied across all reports.

7. The preceding steps will open the blank authoring environment in Cognos Business Insight Advanced.

8. Click on the ⬛ icon to define the layout of the page. Select the ⊞ icon from the drop-down menu to create four quadrants on the dashboard, as shown in the following screenshot:

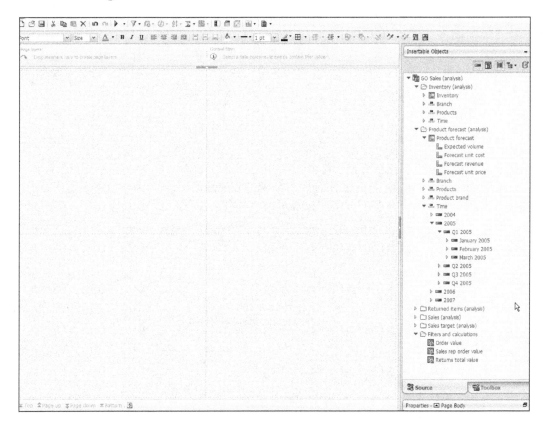

9. Notice the **Go Sales (analysis)** package on the right-hand side under the **Source** tab. Query items can be dragged-and-dropped on the dashboard to define the data to be displayed on the dashboard.

10. Save the dashboard by clicking on the 💾 icon on the Application bar. Save the dashboard by the name of `5825-04-Sample1`.

11. Keep the dashboard open as we will be using it in the following recipes.

How it works...

In this recipe we have started with our first dashboard in Cognos Business Insight Advanced and have defined the basic layout, which will be applied to it.

We can now insert widgets in each of these quadrants to arrive at the final dashboard.

In the following recipes we will continue with the existing setup and insert content to our newly created dashboard.

Inserting a chart widget

In this recipe we will insert a chart widget to the newly created dashboard.

Getting ready

We will use the same setup that we started with in the previous recipe.

How to do it...

To insert a chart widget, perform the following steps:

1. We will now insert a chart in our dashboard—5825-04-Sample1. We already have the dashboard from the previous recipe open in Cognos Business Insight Advanced.

2. In the top-left quadrant, drop the ▦ Chart icon from the **Toolbox** tab. From the **Insert Chart** dialog box, select the **Gauge** chart, as shown in the following screenshot:

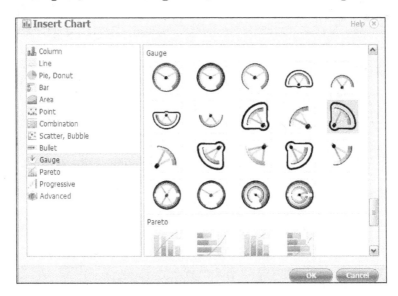

3. From the **Source** tab, drag-and-drop **Expected volume** and **Products** to **Default measure (y-axis)** and **Gauge Axes** respectively, as shown in the following screenshot. The idea is to show product forecast in the term **Expected volume** categorized by **Products** as plotted in the graph in the top-left quadrant of the dashboard.

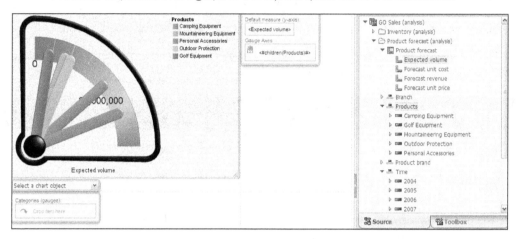

4. Click on the gauge chart in the dashboard area and in the **Properties** pane define the title of the widget as **Expected Volume by Products**, as shown in the following screenshot:

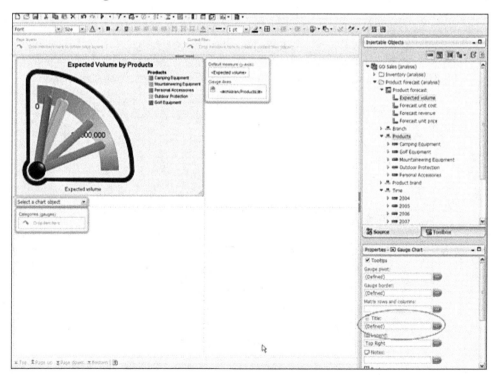

5. Save the dashboard, which now looks like the following screenshot:

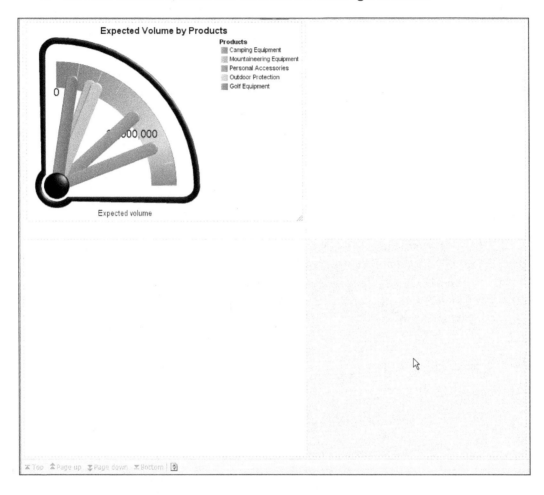

6. Save and keep the dashboard open for the next recipe.

How it works...

In this recipe we have inserted a gauge chart in the dashboard. Different types of charts are available under the **Insert Chart** wizard, as shown earlier in this recipe. It is always desirable to show the information in a chart format, which is easier to read and understand. Selecting the right type of chart is the key.

In the next recipe we will insert a crosstab in the existing dashboard.

Inserting a crosstab widget

In this recipe we will insert a crosstab widget in our dashboard—5825-04-Sample1.

Getting ready

We will use the same setup as in the previous recipe.

How to do it...

To insert a crosstab widget, perform the following steps:

1. In this recipe we will insert a crosstab showing **Forecast revenue** with respect to **Products** and **Time** in the bottom-right quadrant.

2. Drag a **Crosstab** object denoted by ⊞ Crosstab from the **Toolbox** tab and drop it onto the bottom-right quadrant of the dashboard.

3. Drag **Forecast revenue**, **Products**, and **Time** from the metadata package under the **Source** tab and drop them to the center, top, and left-hand side area of the crosstab respectively.

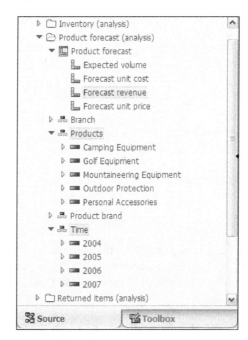

4. Save the resulting dashboard, which now looks like the following screenshot:

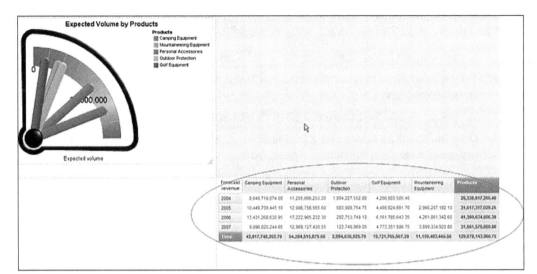

5. Save the dashboard and keep it open for the next recipe.

How it works...

In this recipe we have inserted a crosstab in our dashboard. In the next recipe we will add more widgets to the dashboard and learn more about formatting features.

In the next recipe we will focus more on formatting features, which are available in the tool. We will also add other widgets to make our dashboard complete.

Formatting and arriving at the final layout

In this recipe we will add more content to our dashboard and learn more about formatting features.

Getting ready

We will use the same setup as in the previous recipe.

How to do it...

To format and arrive at the final layout, perform the following steps:

1. We will now add more content to our dashboard—5825-04-Sample1.

2. Drag a chart and drop it in the bottom-right quadrant, just below the **Forecast revenue** crosstab.

3. We will use a **Stacked Cone Bar** chart to render forecast revenue information.

4. Drag the **Chart** object from the **Toolbox** tab and drop it just after the **Forecast revenue** crosstab in the bottom-right quadrant.

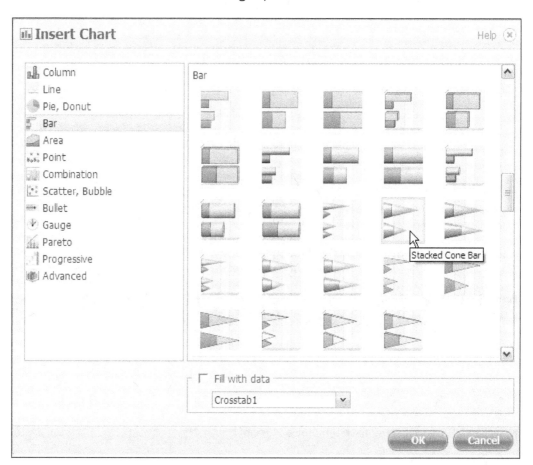

5. Drag **Forecast revenue**, **Products**, and **Time** from the **Source** tab and drop them onto the **Default measure**, **Series**, and **Categories** areas in the chart respectively.

6. From the **Toolbox** tab, drag a **Block** object and drag it just before the crosstab.

7. Drag a **Text** item and drop it inside the preceding block. The text item will be the subtitle for the crosstab. Specify the text as **Forecast revenue by Time for different Products**.

8. Make sure that the block contents are aligned at the center by selecting the block and clicking on the ⊞ icon on the Application bar.

9. Click on the block and adjust **Padding** and **Font** from the **Properties** pane, as shown in the following screenshot:

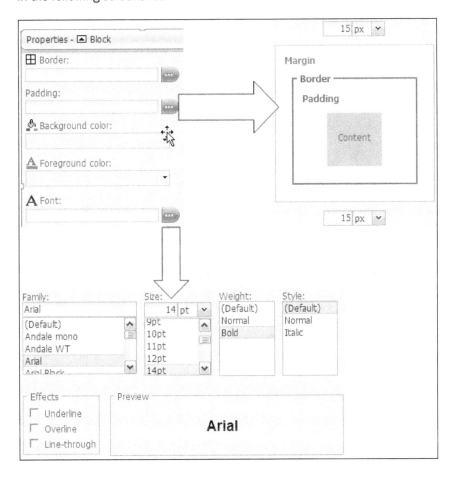

10. Save the dashboard, which now looks like the following screenshot:

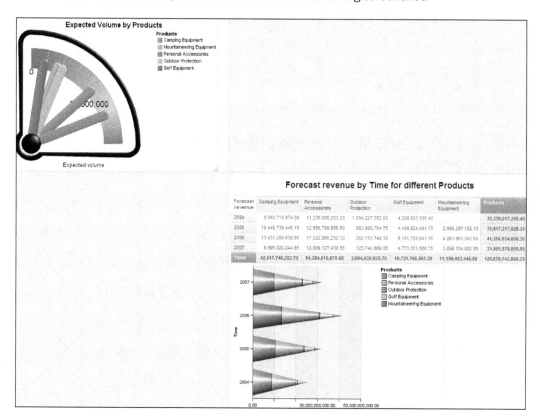

11. On the **Source** tab, click on the **View Metadata Tree** icon denoted by [icon] to display the full package tree. This will change the view in the **Source** tab, as shown in the following screenshot:

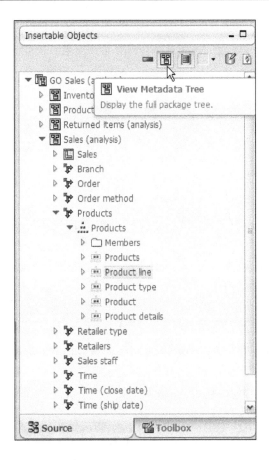

12. Now from the **Toolbox** tab, we will drag a **Table** object to the top-right quadrant. Make sure that the table has two columns and a single row.

13. Apply left and right padding to both the table cells, as shown in the following screenshot:

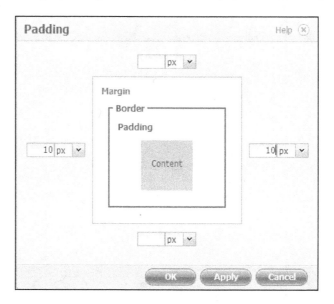

14. Insert a **List** object from the **Toolbox** tab to the left table cell, as shown in the following screenshot:

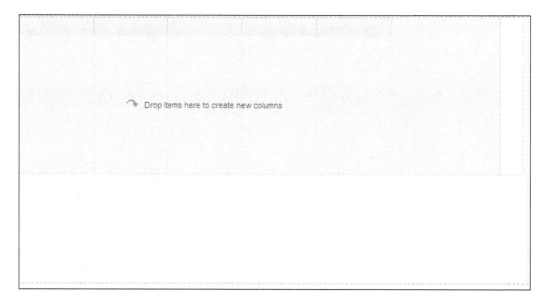

15. Drag levels from the **Sales (analysis)** namespace and drop them into the newly added list. The idea is to display a list showing the actual quantity each year for different products.

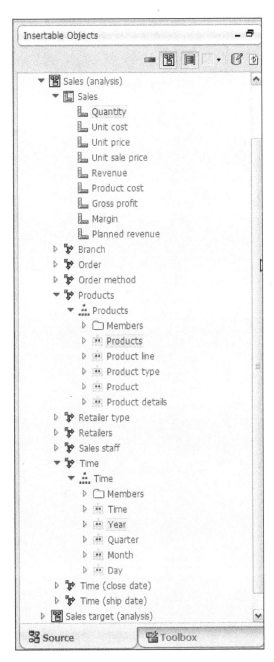

16. Group the list by year by selecting the **Year** column in the list and clicking on the **Group/Ungroup** icon on the Application bar denoted by ▣. The list now looks like the following screenshot:

Year	Product line	Quantity
2004	Camping Equipment	5,895,053
	Personal Accessories	7,572,339
	Outdoor Protection	5,614,356
	Golf Equipment	1,092,982
2004 - Summary		**20,174,730**
2005	Camping Equipment	6,903,764
	Mountaineering Equipment	2,644,713
	Personal Accessories	8,567,357
	Outdoor Protection	4,111,058
	Golf Equipment	1,297,793
2005 - Summary		**23,524,685**
2006	Camping Equipment	8,399,156
	Mountaineering Equipment	3,700,262
	Personal Accessories	10,706,015
	Outdoor Protection	1,599,585
	Golf Equipment	1,536,772
2006 - Summary		**25,941,790**
2007	Camping Equipment	6,103,176
	Mountaineering Equipment	3,555,116
	Personal Accessories	8,061,994
	Outdoor Protection	689,446
	Golf Equipment	1,186,154
2007 - Summary		**19,595,886**
Overall - Summary		89,237,091

17. In the second table cell, on the right-hand side, insert another table with two rows and one column, as shown in the following screenshot:

Year	Product line	Quantity
2004	Camping Equipment	5,895,053
	Personal Accessories	7,572,339
	Outdoor Protection	5,614,356
	Golf Equipment	1,092,982
2004 - Summary		**20,174,730**
2005	Camping Equipment	6,903,764
	Mountaineering Equipment	2,644,713
	Personal Accessories	8,567,357
	Outdoor Protection	4,111,058
	Golf Equipment	1,297,793
2005 - Summary		**23,524,685**
2006	Camping Equipment	8,399,156
	Mountaineering Equipment	3,700,262
	Personal Accessories	10,706,015
	Outdoor Protection	1,599,585
	Golf Equipment	1,536,772
2006 - Summary		**25,941,790**
2007	Camping Equipment	6,103,176
	Mountaineering Equipment	3,555,116
	Personal Accessories	8,061,994
	Outdoor Protection	689,446
	Golf Equipment	1,186,154
2007 - Summary		**19,595,886**
Overall - Summary		**89,237,091**

18. In the first row of the newly created table, insert a **Pie** chart from the **Toolbox** tab. The cursor in the preceding screenshot points to the area where the pie chart needs to be dragged and dropped.

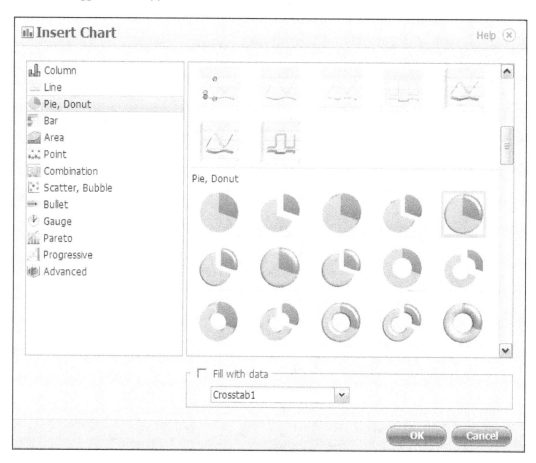

19. Drag **Quantity**, **Product line**, and **Year** from the **Sales (analysis)** namespace in the **Source** tab and drop them onto the **Measure**, **Series**, and **Categories** areas on the pie chart, as shown in the following screenshot:

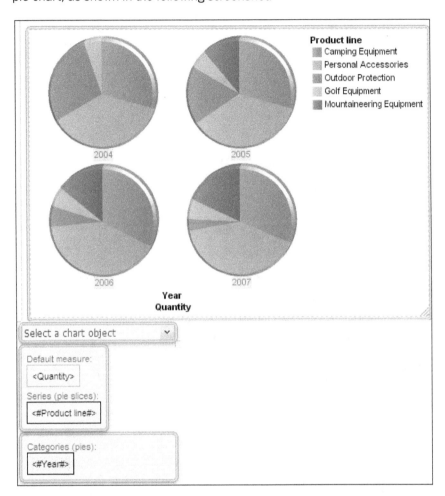

20. Make the table cell contents top-aligned by selecting the table cell and clicking on the ⊟ icon on the Application bar.

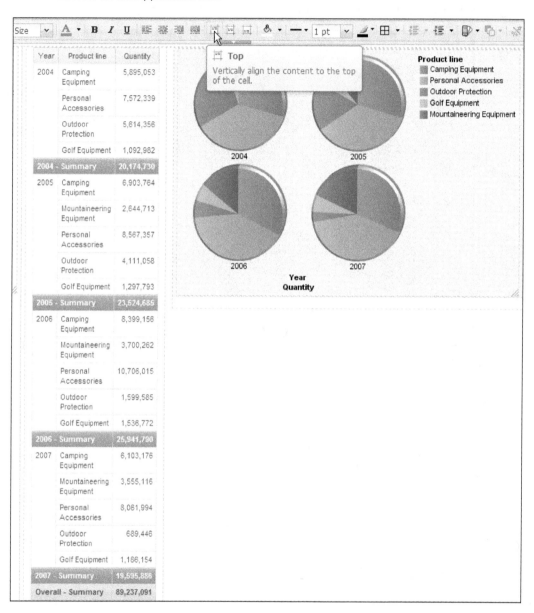

21. Similarly, just below the pie chart in the second row, insert a **Donut** chart, as shown in the following screenshot:

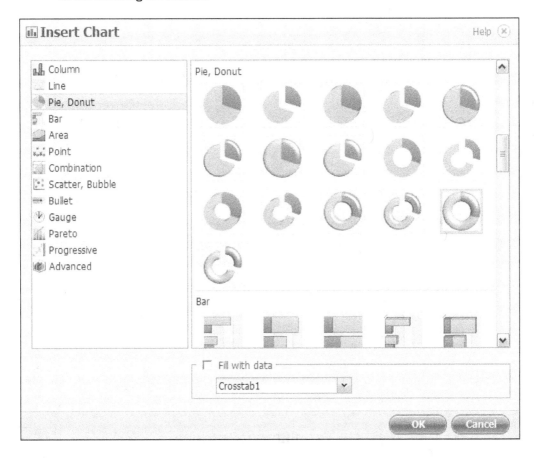

22. Similar to what we did for the pie chart, drag **Revenue**, **Product line**, and **Year** from the **Sales (analysis)** namespace in the **Source** tab, and drop them to the **Measure**, **Series**, and **Categories** areas on the donut chart, as shown in the following screenshot:

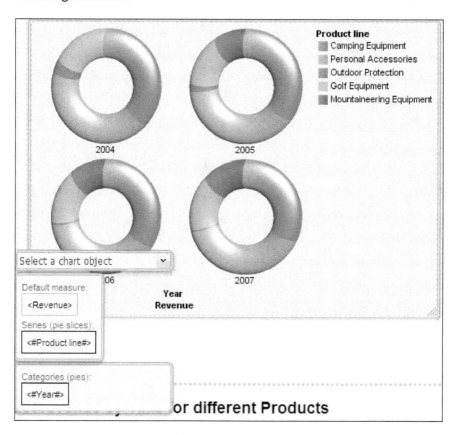

23. Click on the top-left quadrant and click on 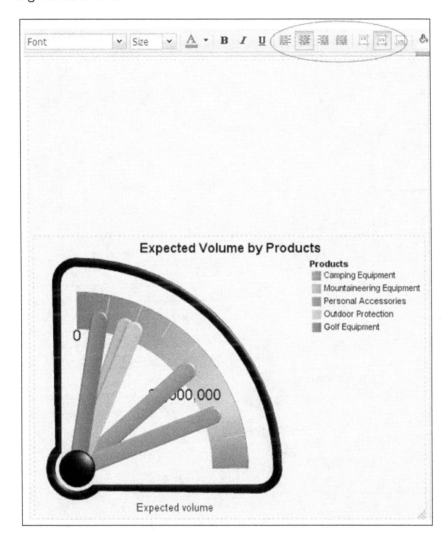 and ⊟ to set the horizontal and vertical alignments to center:

24. Save the dashboard, which now looks like the following screenshot:

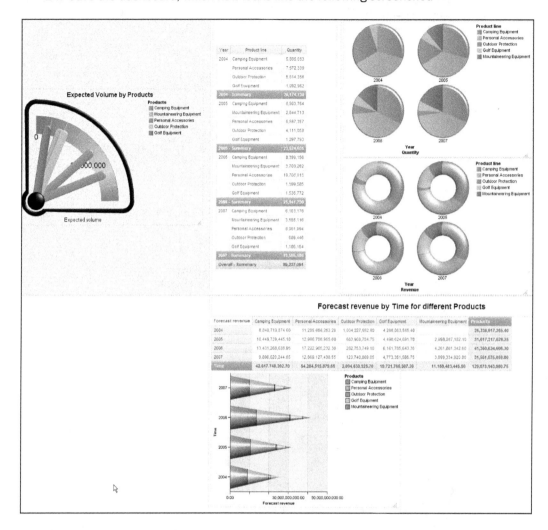

25. Now in the bottom-left quadrant, let us analyze **Gross profit/Revenue** ratio, applicable on actual sales. From the **Toolbox** tab, drag a **Stacked Cylinder** chart and drop it into the bottom-left area.

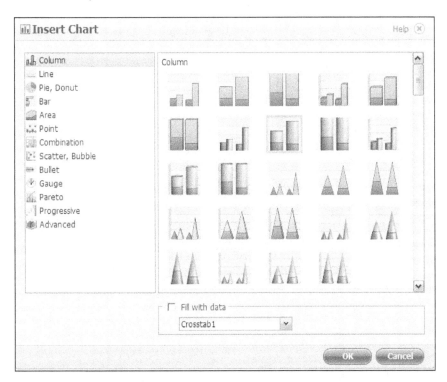

26. From the **Source** tab, drag **Product line** and **Year** and drop them onto **Series** and **Categories** on the chart:

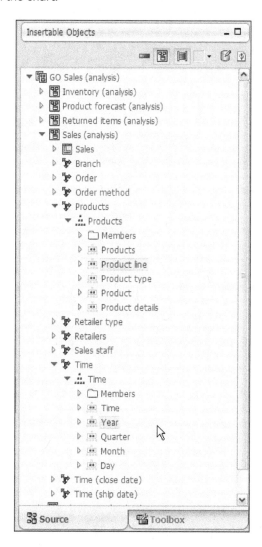

27. From the **Toolbox** tab, drag the **Query Calculation** icon denoted by ▭Query Calculation and drop it under **Default measure** in the chart. It will open the **Create Calculation** dialog box, on which name the calculated data item as **Gross profit/Revenue**.

28. Select the **Calculated measure** checkbox, which indicates we are going to insert a calculated measure in the chart as a default measure:

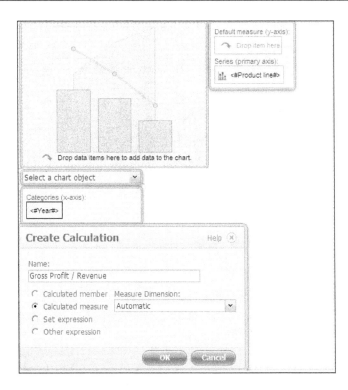

29. It will open an expression editor to create the calculation. Drag-and-drop **Gross profit** and then **Revenue** to define the expression as a division of the two. It is as shown in the following screenshot:

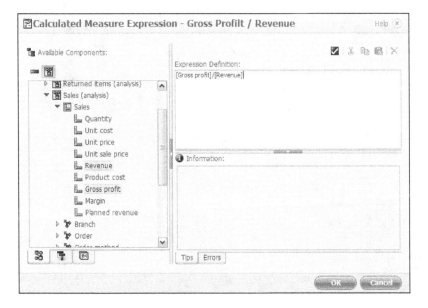

30. The chart is now displayed. Provide a title for the chart as **Gross profit/Revenue by Time for Products**. The chart will now look like the following screenshot:

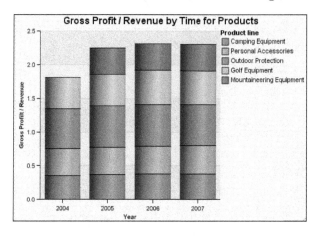

31. Align the contents of the bottom-left chart to center.
32. Save the dashboard. Keep the dashboard open so that we can use that in the next recipe.

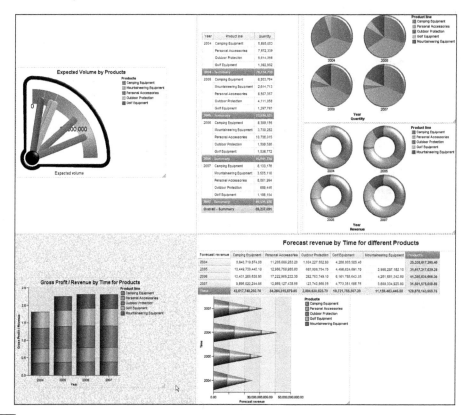

How it works...

In this recipe we have added more content to our first dashboard and applied formatting to customize the look and feel. We have also created a calculated measure and used that in a chart.

In the next recipe we will use the same dashboard we created and see how a user can navigate across a hierarchy.

Performing drill up and drill down

In this recipe we will learn how a user can drill up and drill down through hierarchies and levels.

Navigating from higher level of detail to lower level of detail is called **drill down**. In the same way navigating from lower level of detail to higher level of detail is called **drill up**.

For instance, year-quarter-month-day is a hierarchy with four levels. These levels are year, quarter, month, and day. A user viewing reporting figures for a year might be interested in navigating to individual quarters, which make up that year. Similarly, he/she may want to further drill down to the month level to see monthly level of detail.

In a similar manner a user currently viewing number at day level might be interested in drilling up to view monthly data and so on.

Getting ready

We will use the same setup as in the previous recipe and start with `5825-04-Sample1`, which is already open in Cognos Business Insight Advanced.

 To create drill-up and drill-down reports, it is necessary that the metadata package has dimensions and measures defined along with hierarchies and levels. This type of package is called as a **DMR** or **dimensionally modeled relational** package.

How to do it...

To perform drill up and drill down, go through the following steps:

1. We will now demonstrate the drill functionality using our newly created `5825-04-Sample1` in Cognos Business Insight Advanced. On the Application bar expand the **Data** menu.

2. Select **Drill Options...**, as shown in the following screenshot:

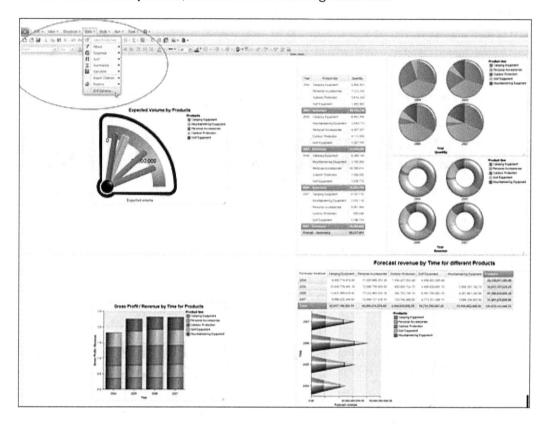

3. It will open the **Drill Options** dialog box to configure drill options. Select the **Allow drill-up and drill-down** checkbox. This will allow a user to drill up and drill down if the underlying package is a DMR:

4. Save the dashboard. It is now drillable. We will now see how we can drill up and drill down in the report.

5. Let us consider the bottom-right quadrant, which is displaying **Forecast revenue by Time for different Products**. We have the stacked cone bar chart here, which has **Time** displayed on the y axis and **Forecast revenue** displayed on the x axis. This gets generated for different product lines, which is represented as a series. We will just focus on the cone for **Time = 2006** here, as shown in the following screenshot:

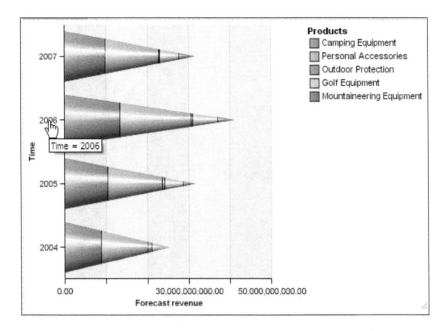

6. Right-click on the caption—**2006** and select the **Drill Down** option from the menu. Alternatively, user can also do a single left-click on the caption—**2006** and it will drill down from **2006**, that is, year level to quarter level.

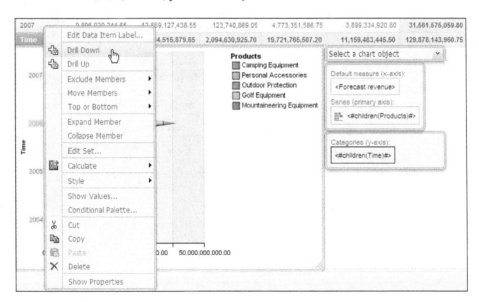

7. The chart view gets changed with the y axis now displaying different quarters in **2006** and the **Forecast revenue** contributions shown for each product line change accordingly.

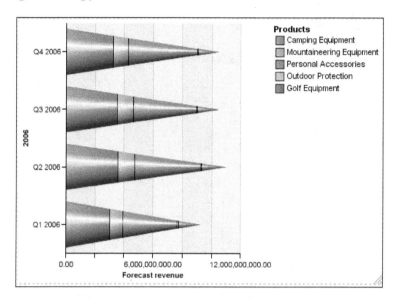

8. This can be drilled down further to month and day level, depending on which levels are defined for the **Time** dimension, in the DMR. We will now again right-click and choose the **Drill Up** option to return to year level, as shown in the following screenshot:

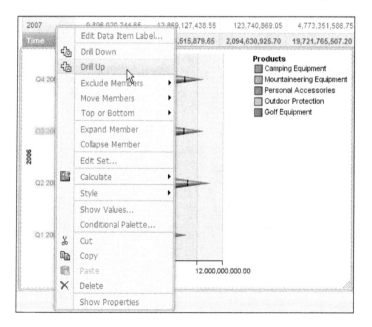

9. Similarly on the donut chart displaying actual **Revenue** by **time** and **Product line**, right-click on the legend **Camping Equipment** and click on **Drill Down** from the **Product line** level to **Product type** level.

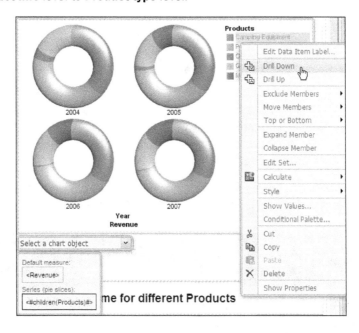

10. The view changes accordingly to show the breakdown for **Camping Equipment**. Here we have performed drill down from **Product line** level to **Product type** level.

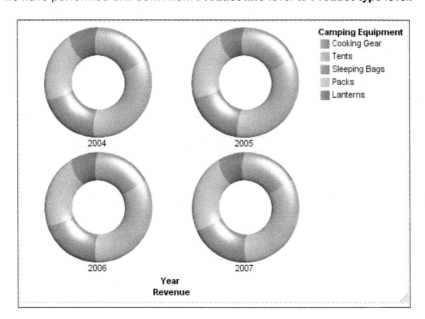

11. Again click on **Drill Up** to return to the original view.

12. Save the dashboard and keep it open in Cognos Business Insight Advanced for the next recipe.

How it works...

We have seen how we can use the DMR package to perform drill up and drill down in the report.

We have dragged-and-dropped levels to the ppropriate areas in widgets on the dashboard. This enables users to navigate from higher level of detail to lower level of detail, based on the levels and their order defined while creating hierarchies. Similar is the case when a user wants to navigate from lower level of detail to higher level of detail, which is called a drill up.

Now we will see how we can apply formatting to various widgets placed on the dashboard based on certain conditions. This is known as **conditional formatting**.

Applying conditional formatting to the dashboard

In this recipe we will see how we can change the look and feel of various widgets placed on the dashboard according to certain conditions.

For instance, coloring crosstab cells based on the numeric values displayed within them, can be termed as conditionally formatting the crosstab widget.

Similarly while rendering bar charts, it is frequently required to show negative values as red color bars while positive values as green color bars. This recipe focuses on such use cases.

Getting ready

We will use the same setup as in the previous recipe and start with 5825-04-Sample1, which is already open in Cognos Business Insight Advanced.

How to do it...

In this recipe we will apply conditional formatting to our newly created dashboard—5825-04-Sample1. Perform the following steps:

1. In the top-right quadrant of the dashboard, select the list displaying **Year**, **Product line**, and **Quantity** and insert two more columns from the **Sales (analysis)** namespace. The two additional columns are **Planned revenue** and **Revenue** in order and are dropped just after the **Quantity** column, as shown in the following screenshot:

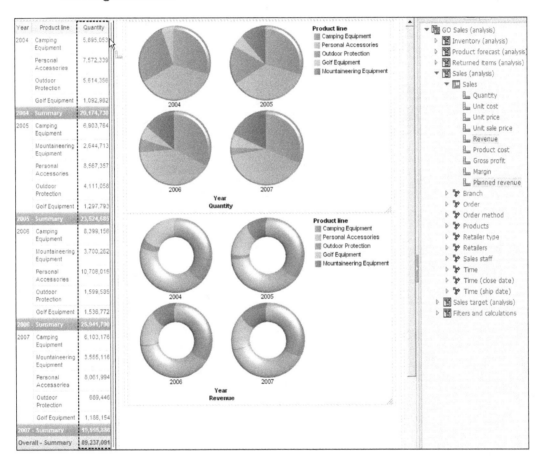

2. The list changes, as shown in the following screenshot:

Year	Product line	Quantity	Planned revenue	Revenue
2004	Camping Equipment	5,895,053	$361,495,088.97	$332,986,338.06
	Personal Accessories	7,572,339	$398,923,067.59	$391,647,093.61
	Outdoor Protection	5,614,356	$38,181,339.98	$36,165,521.07
	Golf Equipment	1,092,982	$169,875,640.98	$153,553,850.98
2004 - Summary		**20,174,730**	**$968,475,137.52**	**$914,352,803.72**
2005	Camping Equipment	6,903,764	$431,970,502.15	$402,757,573.17
	Mountaineering Equipment	2,644,713	$113,363,106.75	$107,099,659.94
	Personal Accessories	8,567,357	$464,458,617.66	$456,323,355.90
	Outdoor Protection	4,111,058	$26,157,261.77	$25,008,574.08
	Golf Equipment	1,297,793	$182,227,978.19	$168,006,427.07
2005 - Summary		**23,524,685**	**$1,218,177,466.52**	**$1,159,195,590.16**
2006	Camping Equipment	8,399,156	$531,010,839.07	$500,382,422.83
	Mountaineering Equipment	3,700,262	$168,584,907.17	$161,039,823.26
	Personal Accessories	10,706,015	$602,227,218.07	$594,009,408.42
	Outdoor Protection	1,599,585	$10,938,440.68	$10,349,175.84
	Golf Equipment	1,536,772	$247,977,474.85	$230,110,270.55
2006 - Summary		**25,941,790**	**$1,560,738,879.84**	**$1,495,891,100.90**
2007	Camping Equipment	6,103,176	$378,648,235.40	$352,910,329.97
	Mountaineering Equipment	3,555,116	$148,620,073.47	$141,520,649.70
	Personal Accessories	8,061,994	$449,774,474.64	$443,693,449.85
	Outdoor Protection	689,446	$4,728,224.46	$4,471,025.26
	Golf Equipment	1,186,154	$190,179,870.09	$174,740,819.29
2007 - Summary		**19,595,886**	**$1,171,950,878.06**	**$1,117,336,274.07**
Overall - Summary		**89,237,091**	**$4,919,342,361.94**	**$4,686,775,768.85**

3. Now we want to insert a calculated column at the end of the last column of the list. The new column will be **ABS(% Diff(Planned Rev, Rev))**, which will tell us by how much percentage **Revenue** differs from **Planned revenue**.

4. From the **Toolbox** tab drag the **Query Calculation** icon and drop it at the end of the list after the **Revenue** column.

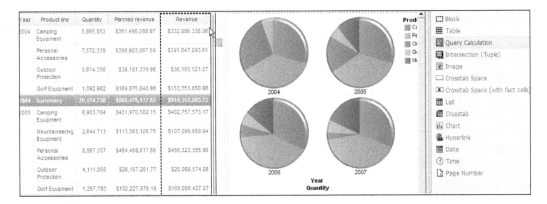

5. In the **Create Calculation** dialog box, define the name of the new column. Also configure it to be a calculated measure by selecting the **Calculated measure** checkbox to be computed at **Measure Dimension–Sales (analysis) | Sales**, as shown in the following screenshot:

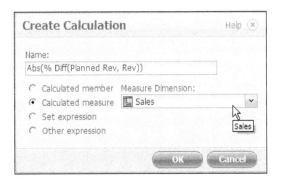

6. Define the calculation in the calculated measure—**Expression Definition**, as shown in the following screenshot:

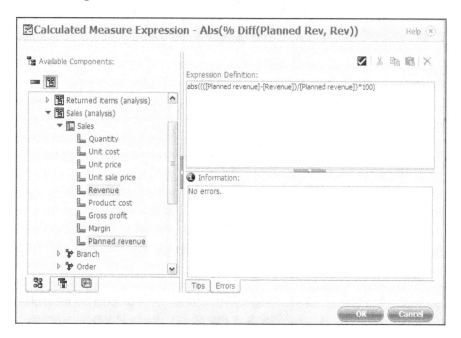

7. Click on the **OK** button and see how the list changes:

Year	Product line	Quantity	Planned revenue	Revenue	Abs(% Diff (Planned Rev, Rev))
2004	Camping Equipment	5,895,053	$361,495,088.97	$332,986,338.08	7.88634529
	Personal Accessories	7,572,339	$398,923,067.59	$391,647,093.61	1.82390405
	Outdoor Protection	5,614,356	$38,181,339.98	$36,165,521.07	5.27959184
	Golf Equipment	1,092,982	$169,875,640.98	$153,553,850.98	9.60808148
	Mountaineering Equipment				
2004 - Summary		20,174,730	$968,475,137.52	$914,352,803.72	5.58840715
2005	Camping Equipment	6,903,764	$431,970,502.15	$402,757,573.17	6.76271385
	Personal Accessories	8,567,357	$464,458,617.66	$456,323,355.90	1.75155793
	Outdoor Protection	4,111,058	$26,157,261.77	$25,008,574.08	4.39146765
	Golf Equipment	1,297,793	$182,227,978.19	$168,006,427.07	7.80426324
	Mountaineering Equipment	2,644,713	$113,363,106.75	$107,099,659.94	5.52511923
2005 - Summary		23,524,685	$1,218,177,466.52	$1,159,195,590.16	4.84181312

8. Clearly, the last column shows the absolute values of the percentage difference between what was planned and what is displayed in actuality.

9. Now we want to conditionally change the background color of the newly added column depending on the numeric range in which the column value falls.

10. Select the last column, that is, **Abs(% Diff(Planned Rev, Rev))** and click on **Conditional Styles...**, as shown in the following screenshot:

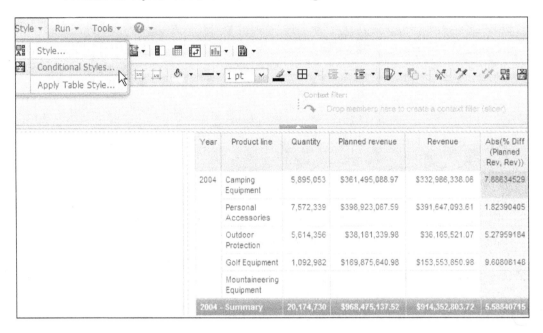

11. Create a new conditional style by clicking on **New Conditional Style...**, as shown in the following screenshot:

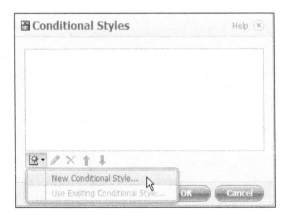

12. Select the newly computed column in a window, as shown in the following screenshot.

13. Based on the selected column values, the condition will be computed and styles will be applied to different cells accordingly.

14. Click on ▨ to define threshold values, which define different numeric ranges.

15. Click on ▱ to define formatting for every range.

16. Define conditional style for each numeric range in the **Conditional Style – Numeric Range** window, as shown in the following screenshot:

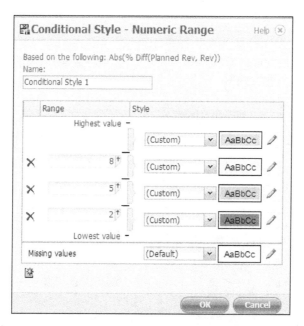

17. Click on the **OK** button and see how the conditional formatting defined in the preceding screenshot has changed the look and feel of the list:

Year	Product line	Quantity	Planned revenue	Revenue	Abs(% Diff (Planned Rev, Rev))
2004	Camping Equipment	5,895,053	$361,495,088.97	$332,986,338.06	7.88634529
	Personal Accessories	7,572,339	$398,923,067.59	$391,647,093.61	1.82390405
	Outdoor Protection	5,614,356	$38,181,339.98	$36,165,521.07	5.27959184
	Golf Equipment	1,092,982	$169,875,640.98	$153,553,850.98	9.60808148
	Mountaineering Equipment				
2004 - Summary		**20,174,730**	**$968,475,137.52**	**$914,352,803.72**	**5.58840715**
2005	Camping Equipment	6,903,764	$431,970,502.15	$402,757,573.17	6.76271385
	Personal Accessories	8,567,357	$464,458,617.66	$456,323,355.90	1.75155793
	Outdoor Protection	4,111,058	$26,157,261.77	$25,008,574.08	4.39146765
	Golf Equipment	1,297,793	$182,227,978.19	$168,006,427.07	7.80426324
	Mountaineering Equipment	2,644,713	$113,363,106.75	$107,099,659.94	5.52511923
2005 - Summary		**23,524,685**	**$1,218,177,466.52**	**$1,159,195,590.16**	**4.84181312**
2006	Camping Equipment	8,399,156	$531,010,839.07	$500,382,422.83	5.76794558
	Personal Accessories	10,706,015	$602,227,218.07	$594,009,408.42	1.36456962
	Outdoor Protection	1,599,585	$10,938,440.68	$10,349,175.84	5.38710093
	Golf Equipment	1,536,772	$247,977,474.85	$230,110,270.55	7.20517229
	Mountaineering Equipment	3,700,262	$168,584,907.17	$161,039,823.26	4.47553938
2006 - Summary		**25,941,790**	**$1,560,738,879.84**	**$1,495,891,100.90**	**4.15494096**
2007	Camping Equipment	6,103,176	$378,648,235.40	$352,910,329.97	6.79731292
	Personal Accessories	8,061,994	$449,774,474.64	$443,693,449.85	1.35201643
	Outdoor Protection	689,446	$4,728,224.46	$4,471,025.26	5.43965715
	Golf Equipment	1,186,154	$190,179,870.09	$174,740,819.29	8.1181309
	Mountaineering Equipment	3,555,116	$148,620,073.47	$141,520,649.70	4.77689427
2007 - Summary		**19,595,886**	**$1,171,950,878.06**	**$1,117,336,274.07**	**4.66014447**
Overall - Summary		89,237,091	$4,919,342,361.94	$4,686,775,768.85	4.72759519

18. Save the dashboard and it now looks like the following screenshot:

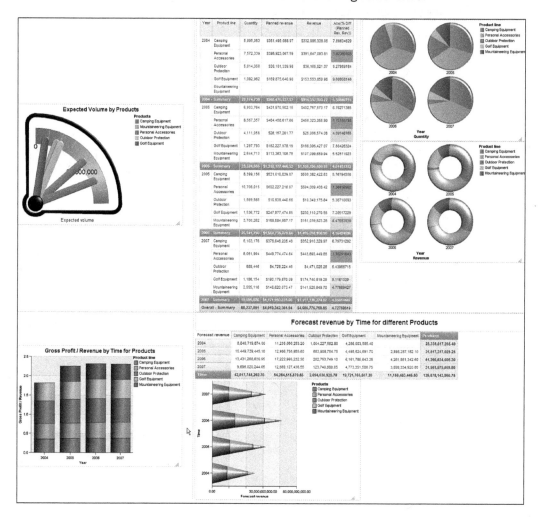

How it works...

We have used our newly created dashboard and applied conditional formatting on top of that.

Changing the coloring scheme based on a condition is just one of the use cases, which can be achieved by conditional formatting. Objects can also be rendered and hidden based on a condition using conditional formatting.

In this recipe we defined a calculation based on the existing data in the list and colored the list cells in the column based on the numeric ranges in which the actual value falls.

At the end of this chapter we created our own dashboard and used various features provided in IBM Cognos Business Insight Advanced ourselves.

There's more...

In later chapters we will use the dashboard along with the existing sample dashboards to design more extensive dashboards in Cognos Business Insight. Unlike dashboards and reports created in Cognos Business Insight Advanced, such extensive dashboards are not limited to just a single package and can display data from multiple packages. This helps to provide a unified, pigeon-hole view of the enterprise-wide data, scattered across different domains and data sources.

Authors could create different domain-specific and package-specific complex reports and dashboards in Cognos Business Insight Advanced or in Cognos Report Studio. Individual widgets placed on them can then be used independently to design an enterprise-wide dashboard showing data across domains and packages.

5
Creating Dashboards in Cognos Business Insight

In this chapter we will be:

- ▶ Creating a dashboard in Cognos Business Insight
- ▶ Applying filters in Cognos Business Insight
- ▶ Configuring widget controls in Cognos Business Insight

Introduction

In the previous chapter we learned how we can create dashboards in Cognos Business Insight Advanced. We also saw the basic graphical user interface that Cognos Business Insight has to design dashboards.

In this chapter we will see how we can create dashboards in Cognos Business Insight using existing reports and dashboards.

We will use the already installed samples and the dashboard we created in the previous chapter on Cognos Business Insight Advanced.

Creating a dashboard in Cognos Business Insight

In this recipe we will be creating a dashboard in Cognos Business Insight. We will use the `5825-04-Sample1` dashboard we have created in the previous chapter on Cognos Business Insight Advanced and the `GO Sales` and `GO Data Warehouse` samples we have already installed.

Getting ready

IBM Cognos BI Server should be started. The `GO Data Warehouse` and `GO Sales` samples should be installed.

How to do it...

To create a dashboard in Cognos Business Insight, perform the following steps:

1. Log on to **IBM Cognos Connection** and create a new folder with name of **IBM Cognos Business Insight Samples**, as shown in the following screenshot:

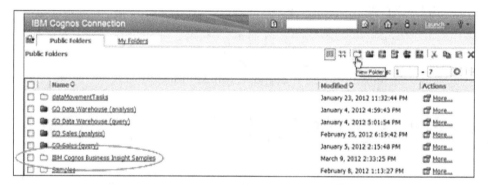

2. Navigate inside the newly created folder and open **Business Insight** from the **Launch** menu, as shown in the following screenshot:

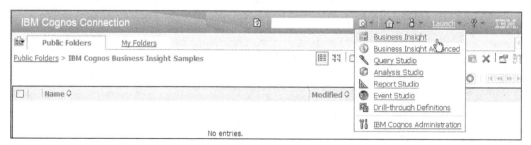

3. Click on the **Create New** button to open the Cognos Business Insight graphical interface.

4. On the right-hand side pane, note the dashboard—**5825-04-Sample1** that we created in the previous chapter on Cognos Business Insight Advanced. When we expand that, it shows the list of widgets that are placed on it. For instance, we have **List1**, **Pie Chart1**, and **Pie Chart2** placed on the **5825-04-Sample1** dashboard.

5. When we drag-and-drop a widget on a dashboard, for instance a **List** on **5825-04-Sample1**, Cognos provides a unique name to that, for instance **List1**. Similarly, as we have used a pie chart at two places on **5825-04-Sample1**, Cognos has named them as **Pie Chart1** and **Pie Chart2**. The names given are specific to the dashboard.

6. These widget instances (for example, **List1**, **Pie Chart1**, **Pie Chart2**, and so on), which are shown in the Cognos Business Insight interface when we expand the host dashboard (for example, **5825-04-Sample1** listed on the right-hand side pane in the following screenshot), can be dragged-and-dropped in Cognos Business Insight, and reused to design new enterprise dashboards. The work area where the objects need to be dropped to create dashboards is called **canvas**, which has its left and centre areas empty, as shown in the following screenshot:

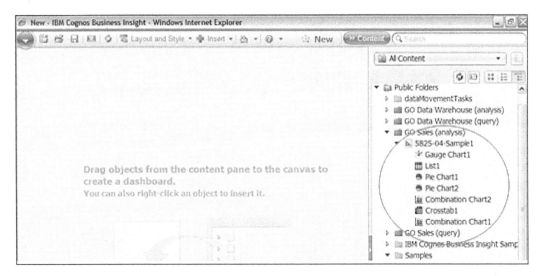

7. Close the Cognos Business Insight interface and in Cognos Connection, navigate to **Public Folders | GO Sales (analysis)** to open **5825-04-Sample1** in Cognos Business Insight Advanced, as shown in the screenshot just after the next step.

8. Specify the title in the **Properties** pane for each widget. For instance, we provide **Chart Title** for the pie chart placed on the bottom-right corner of the dashboard, as shown in the following screenshot:

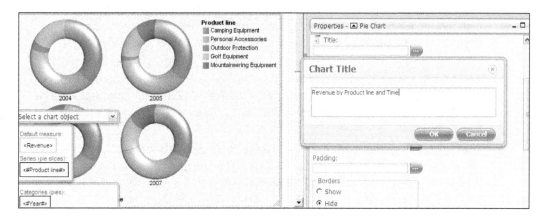

9. Similarly, provide a title for each widget. Save and close the Cognos Business Unit Advanced interface.

10. In Cognos Connection, navigate to **Public Folders | IBM Cognos Business Insight Samples** and from the **Launch** menu, open **Business Insight**. Click on the **Create New** button to create a new dashboard.

11. On the right-hand side pane, notice the various objects available under **5825-04-Sample1**, each representing a widget instance we have placed on the dashboard.

12. Right-click on **Gauge Chart1** and then click on **Insert**, as shown in the following screenshot:

13. This will insert the **Expected Volume by Products** chart on the dashboard, as shown in the following screenshot. The widget can be clicked to select, dragged, and moved to any available space on the canvas.

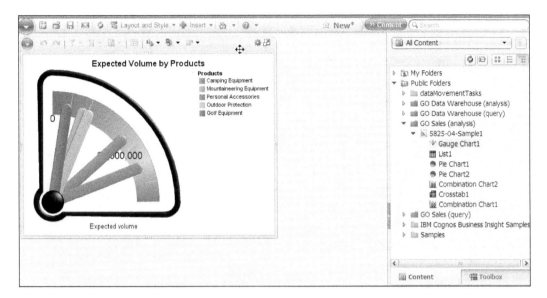

14. Save the dashboard as **5825-01-Sample2** at the location **Public Folders | IBM Cognos Business Insight Samples**. Navigate to **IBM Cognos Connection** to locate the newly saved dashboard, as shown in the following screenshot:

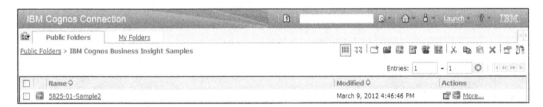

15. Return to **5825-01-Sample2** and open that in Cognos Business Insight. Drag the **Recruitment by department** object from the **Recruitment Success** report, which is available at the location **Public Folders | Samples | Models | GO Data Warehouse (query) | Business Insight Source Reports**, and drop the object on the canvas beside the existing **Expected Volume by Products** chart, as shown in the following screenshot:

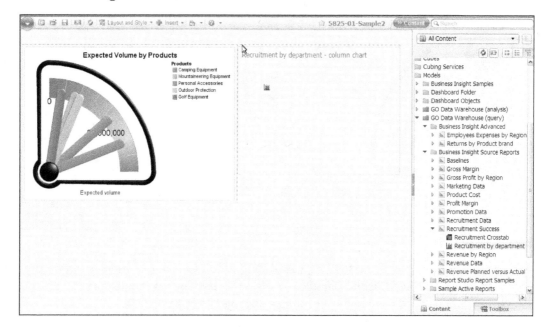

16. This will place the column chart on the canvas. Hence, it can be seen that objects from altogether different reports can be used to create a singular view easily. These objects can be formatted and presented to the users in the best possible format.

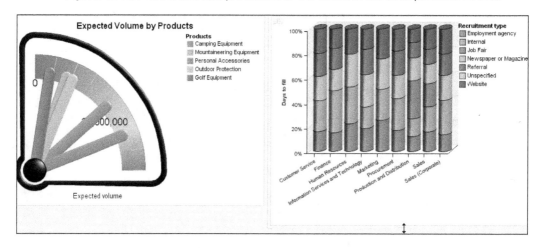

17. Save by clicking on the ⊟ icon on the Application bar.

18. Similarly, insert the **Revenue by Order method** pie chart from the **Revenue Data** report.

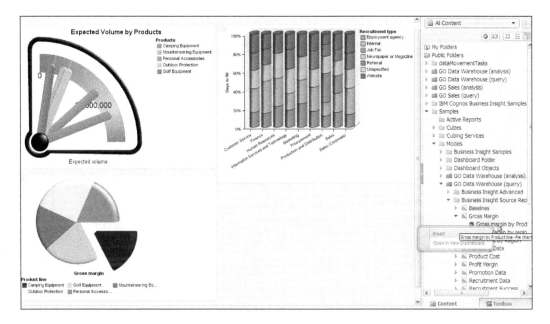

19. Insert the **Planned vs actual** combination chart from the **Revenue Planned versus Actual** report and **Baselines Chart** from the **Baselines** report, as shown in the following screenshot:

20. The dashboard now looks like the following screenshot:

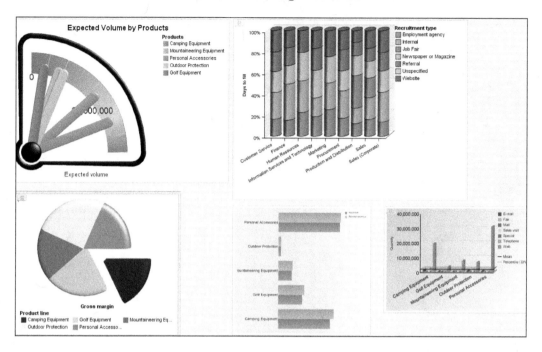

21. Save the dashboard and keep it open for the next recipe.

How it works...

In this recipe we saw how various objects that we already created can be reused to design a dashboard.

Report authors can create reports and dashboards in Cognos Report Studio and Cognos Business Insight Advanced. Business users can log on to Cognos Business Insight and create their own dashboards simply by dragging-and-dropping the objects from already created reports and dashboards in Cognos Business Insight. They can be saved and distributed in different ways, which we will discuss in the later chapter.

Now we will apply filters to the dashboard we have just created. In later chapters we will also learn about ways in which dashboards can be accessed and distributed to different users and groups.

Applying filters in Cognos Business Insight

In this recipe we will apply filters to narrow down the data displayed on the dashboard. We will learn how we can limit the amount of data shown in the widgets by applying appropriate filter on each of them.

We will use the 5825-01-Sample2 dashboard we had created in the previous recipe.

Getting ready

We already have the dashboard—5825-01-Sample2, which we created in the previous recipe, open in the Cognos Business Insight interface. We have also saved the dashboard at the location **Public Folders | IBM Cognos Business Insight Samples** on Cognos Connection.

How to do it...

Now we will refine the data appearing on the 5825-01-Sample2 dashboard using filters provided on the Cognos Business Insight interface. Perform the following steps:

1. Click on the **Toolbox** tab. The various objects that can be inserted onto the dashboard are displayed, as shown in the following screenshot:

2. Let us now drag the **Select Value Filter** object and drop it on to the canvas to open the **Properties – Select Value Filter** dialog box to configure the filter.

3. We want to apply a filter to the **Planned vs actual** chart and **Baselines Chart**. The filter would show list of years for which data has been consolidated and displayed in the charts. The user would be able to select one or more years under the **Year** section, as shown in the following screenshot:

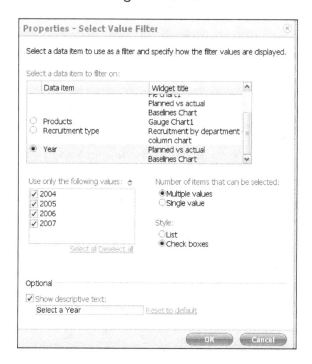

4. Note that the select value filter appears on the dashboard showing the list of years. All the possible values under the **Year** section, which can appear on the chart are shown in the preceding screenshot. These are distinct year values from the database. One or more of these can be selected or deselected to refine data based on which the two charts are then rendered.

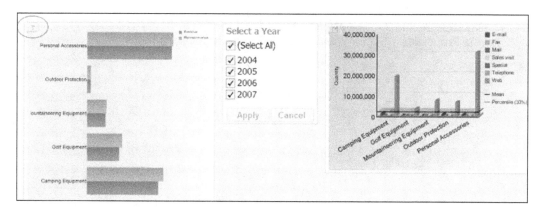

5. Note the ⊡ icon circled in red, which denotes that one or more filters are applied to the chart.

6. Let us now select **2006** and **2007** from the **Select a Year** list prompt, click on **Apply**, and see how that changes the data displayed in the two charts:

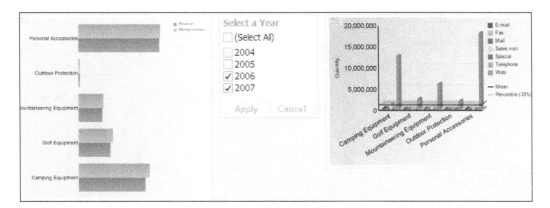

7. Note the change in the numeric range in which the bars fall now. Save the dashboard.

8. We will now drag-and-drop another **Select Value Filter** object and apply it to the **Expected Volume by Products** gauge chart. The user should be able to select a product under the **Select a Product** section, apply it using the **Apply** button, and see the updated chart, as shown in the following screenshot:

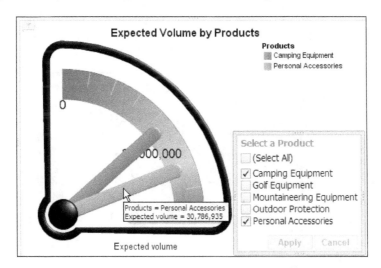

9. Save the dashboard. We will now drag-and-drop the **Slider Filter** object from the **Toolbox** tab to the canvas. As shown in the following screenshot, configure the slider filter to apply that to the **Recruitment by department** column chart, so that user can select a range of values for **Days to fill** under the **Data Item** section:

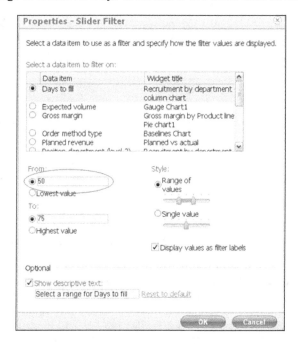

10. Note that the custom range can be defined for the data item. Shown in the following screenshot is the slider filter when applied to the chart:

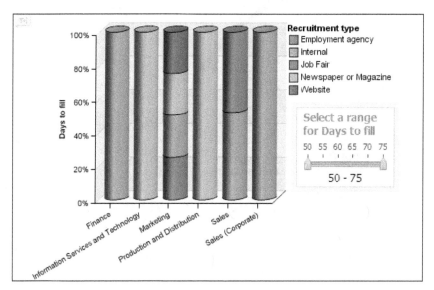

11. Let us now adjust the slider bar to filter the data appearing on the chart, with the **Days to fill** values in the range of **60** to **70**. The chart changes accordingly. Save the dashboard.

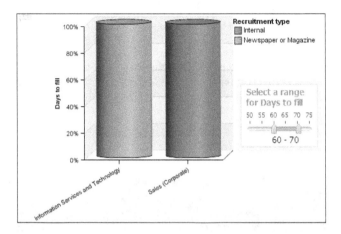

12. Now we have arrived at the final layout of our dashboard, as shown in the following screenshot. Note that each of these widgets can be dragged and moved to different areas on the interface, to rearrange and to give the desired look and feel. The user can also resize these widgets by dragging in or dragging out the widget corners.

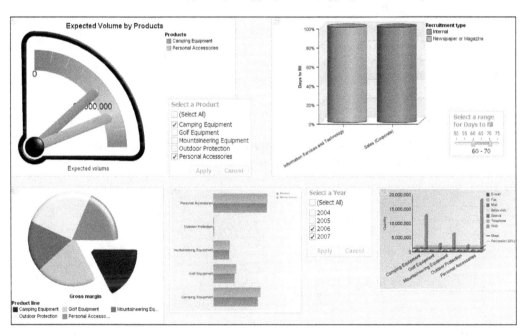

13. Keep the dashboard open for the next recipe.

How it works...

In this recipe we have used filter controls to refine the data appearing in various widgets on the dashboard. Different filters can be applied to different widgets, and hence, the user can choose to view data according to his/her preferences.

> Best practice would be to group the filter close to the widgets it affects. This will avoid confusion, especially if the dashboard is not authored by the end user.

The next recipe will take a closer look at the widget controls and how each of these can be further customized independently.

Configuring widget controls to customize the dashboard

In this recipe we will customize the look and feel of the dashboard we have created by adjusting widget controls individually.

Getting ready

Keep the `5825-01-Sample2` dashboard we have created and worked upon in the previous recipes, open in Cognos Business Insight.

How to do it...

To configure widget controls to customize the dashboard, perform the following steps:

1. On the dashboard adjust the **Days to fill** slider filter for the numeric range between **55** and **75**, as shown in the following screenshot:

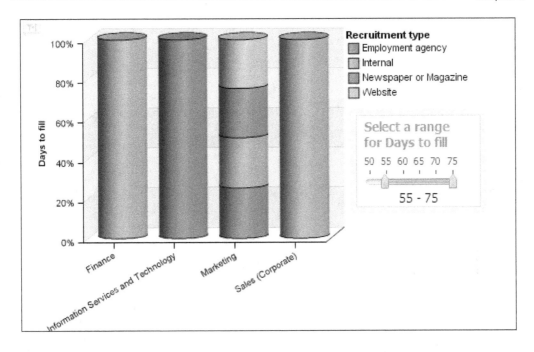

2. Click on the **Recruitment type** column chart and focus the mouse to expose the Widget toolbar. This will push the slider filter to the background. Widgets can be dragged and moved on the dashboard to expose the filter again.

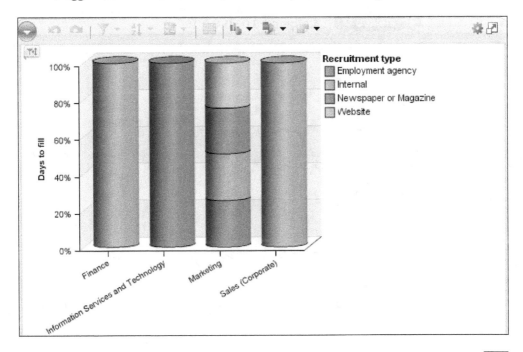

3. Click on the 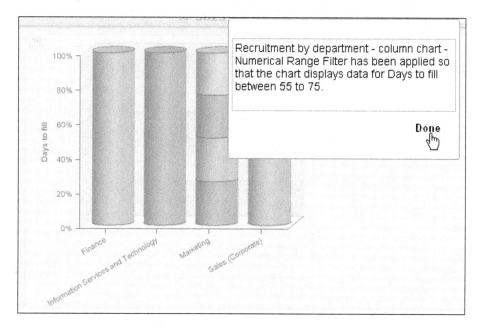 icon to insert a comment on the chart, as shown in the following screenshot:

4. Enter the comment in the textbox and click on the **Done** button. The comment will be shown as a red tooltip on which mouse can be hovered to view the comment text, as shown in the following screenshot:

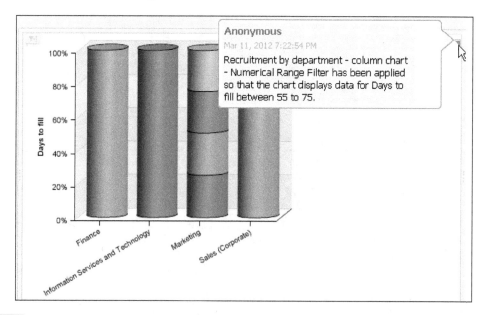

5. Save the dashboard. Now click on the **Expected Volume by Products** gauge chart. Click on the ![icon] icon to change the chart color palette, as shown in the following screenshot:

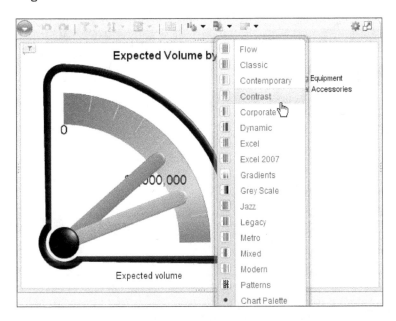

6. As seen in the preceding screenshot the gauge chart has come above the checkbox filter that is not visible now. Click on ![icon], and click on the **Send to Back** menu option to push the chart in background and expose the filter, as shown in the following screenshot:

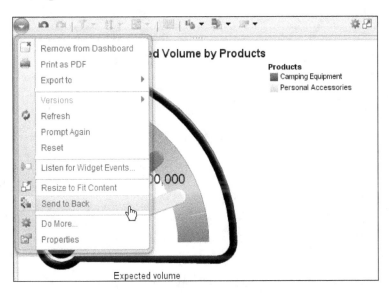

7. Save the dashboard. The dashboard now looks like the following screenshot:

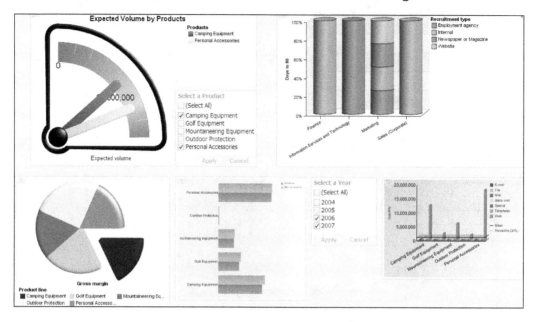

8. In the **Select a Product** section, select all products and click on **Apply**. Note that the color palette of **Expected Volume by Products** has changed, as shown in the following screenshot:

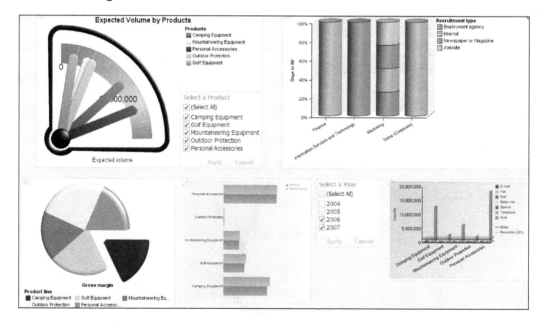

9. Now save the dashboard and close all windows.

How it works...

In this chapter we saw how we can design a dashboard on Cognos Business Insight using existing objects and interface components. We saw how we can customize the look and feel of the dashboard and refine the data shown on the dashboard.

In the next chapter we will see how we can share and distribute the dashboard in different ways, depending on the user's requirements.

6
Sharing and Collaborating with Other Users

In this chapter we will be:

- ▶ Collaborating with other users
- ▶ Sharing Cognos content – adding portal pages to Cognos Connection
- ▶ Sharing Cognos content – adding reports as portal tabs
- ▶ Sharing the Cognos Business Insight dashboard

Introduction

In this chapter we will learn about various modes of communication in Cognos, which can take place between different users, who have varying needs. This involves placing live news feeds from external sources on the dashboard, so that the information is broadcast to all the dashboard users. Users can collaborate with each other using the e-mail functionality provided in Cognos. We will also cover how we can share dashboard and reports among various users by placing Cognos content on portals.

The first recipe talks about collaboration among users using news feeds and e-mails.

Collaborating with other users

In this recipe we will see how users can collaborate with each other using widgets in the Cognos Business Insight interface. We will open the 5825-01-Sample2 dashboard we had created in *Chapter 5, Creating Dashboards in Cognos Business Insight*. We will open the dashboard in the Cognos Business Insight interface and discuss in detail the following functionalities:

- ▸ **RSS Feed**
- ▸ **My Inbox**
- ▸ **Email Link**

Getting ready

Make sure that IBM Cognos 10 BI server is running. The GO Sales and GO Data Warehouse samples should be installed.

How to do it...

To collaborate with other users, perform the following steps:

1. Log on to Cognos Connection.
2. Navigate to **Public Folders | IBM Cognos Business Insight Samples**.
3. Open **5825-01-Sample2** in the Cognos Business Insight interface.
4. In the **Toolbox** tab we have the **RSS Feed** widget, as shown in the screenshot just after the following information box.

> The **RSS Feed** widget is useful for saving or retaining updated information on websites that a user frequently visits or websites that are added as favorites. It uses an XML code, which continuously scans the content on a certain site in search of new information and transmits any information updates.
>
> The **RSS Feed** allows a user to show the content of a **Real Simple Syndication** (**RSS**) or an Atom News Feed, which is specified by a **Uniform Resource Locator** (**URL**).

5. The RSS or Atom Feed URL must be added to the trusted domain list as defined in the Cognos Configuration tool.

 For more information, refer to *IBM Cognos 10 BI Installation and Configuration Guide* or contact the system administrator.

6. Drag the **RSS Feed** widget from the **Toolbox** menu and drop it on the dashboard.

7. The properties of the **RSS Feed** widget can be configured as required, as shown in the following screenshot:

8. The following table specifies the most important properties and their description:

Serial number	Property	Description
1	**URL**	This specifies the URL address that identifies the RSS or Atom channel feed.
2	**Options**	These Specify the display options for the RSS or Atom feed.
3	**Maximum number of entries to display**	This specifies the maximum number of feed links to display in the widget.
4	**Open links**	This specifies how the links in the **RSS Feed** widget are opened.

9. Now we will discuss the **My Inbox** widget, which is useful in collaborating with other users. This is available under the **Tools** pane, as shown in the following screenshot:

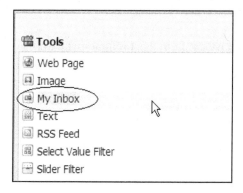

The **My Inbox** widget can be used to show RSS feed of the secure approval requests, ad-hoc tasks, and notification requests from **My Inbox** in Cognos Connection. Using the **My Inbox** widget, a user can view various requests and tasks assigned to him/her through Cognos. The **RSS Feed** widget instead shows the updates from external sources not specific to a user.

The **My Inbox** widget in Cognos Connection, and how tasks and requests can be sent to a user is beyond the scope of this book.

10. The properties of the **Email Link** widget can be specified by clicking on the **Properties** menu item on the Widget toolbar, as shown in the following screenshot:

11. Selecting the **Properties** menu option in the preceding screenshot will open the **Properties – My Inbox** dialog box, which can be used to configure the **Email Link** widget:

12. Refer to the following table for properties under the **RSS Feed** tab:

Serial number	Property	Description
1	**URL**	This specifies the URL address of the RSS feed link to **My Inbox**. The URL address is predefined and should not be changed.
2	**Options**	These Specify the display options for the RSS feed.
3	**Maximum number of entries to display**	This specifies the maximum number of feed links to display in the widget.
4	**Open links**	This specifies how the links in the **My Inbox** widget are opened.

13. Now we will move to the **Email Link** icon denoted by ✉, which is available on the Application bar. It can be used to send dashboard links to other users.

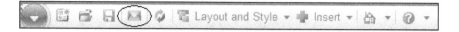

14. The **Email Link** icon when clicked, will invoke the e-mail setup configured on the server and the dashboard link will be sent to other users through e-mail.

How it works...

We have seen three functionalities available in Cognos Business Insight that can be used in various ways to interact with other users as well as external sources.

While RSS feeds are commonly used to stay in sync with the latest changes in web content, **My Inbox** can be configured to receive the latest notifications and alerts.

We have also seen how users can e-mail the dashboard links to other people using previously setup mail clients.

The next recipe will focus on sharing reports and dashboard views, so that other users can log on to Cognos Connection and view the data without navigating too much.

Sharing Cognos content – adding portal pages to Cognos Connection

Multiple portal pages can be added on Cognos Connection. On a portal page, IBM Cognos content (such as reports and dashboards), utilities (such as URLs and bookmarks), and third-party portlets can be added. Users can log on to Cognos Connection and view all the content placed on the portal pages directly, without navigating to directories and folder structures.

Security can be added so that portal pages can be made available to a group of users in an organization in a controlled manner.

In this recipe we will see how we can create a portal page, add content on it, and share it with other users.

Getting ready

Make sure that IBM Cognos 10 server is running. We will use the GO Sales and GO Data Warehouse samples to perform this recipe.

How to do it...

To add portal pages to Cognos Connection, perform the following steps:

1. Log on to Cognos Connection and navigate to **Public Folders**. Create a folder called **My Portal**. We will now create our portal into this folder.

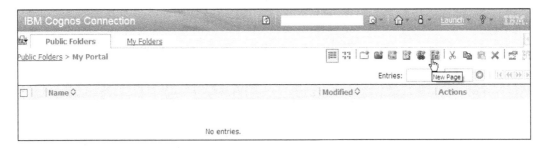

2. Click on the ▦ icon on the Application bar to add a new page.

3. It will open the **Specify a name and description – New page wizard** window to specify a name and location for this entry. We can also specify a description and screen tip under the **Description** and **Screen tip** sections respectively:

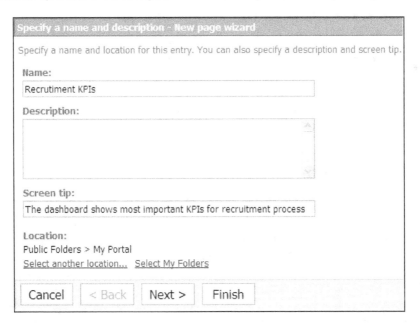

4. The next screen defines the layout of the newly added portal. Select ⊙▥ under **Number of columns**.

5. Adjust **Column width** to **30%** and **70%** for the left and right-hand side panes respectively, as shown in the following screenshot:

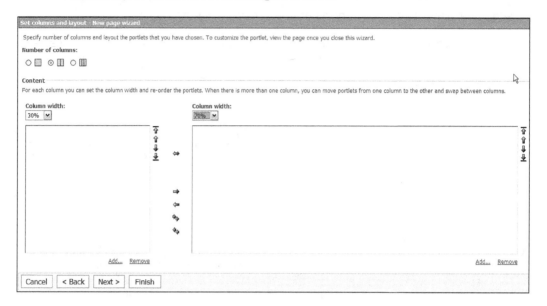

6. Click on the **Add...** link at the bottom of each pane to select and add portlets to each of these pane areas:

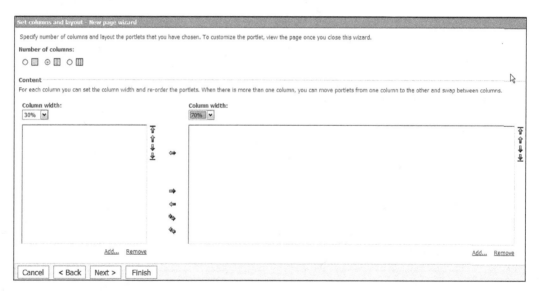

7. In the **Select portlets (Navigate) – New page wizard** window, four types of portlets are available. Navigate to **IBM Cognos Content** and select the **IBM Cognos Navigator** portlet, as shown in the following screenshot. Click on **OK** to add the **IBM Cognos Navigator** portlet to the left-hand side pane:

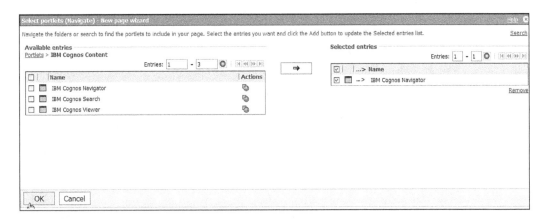

8. Similarly, add an **IBM Cognos Viewer** portlet to the right-hand side pane, as shown in the following screenshot:

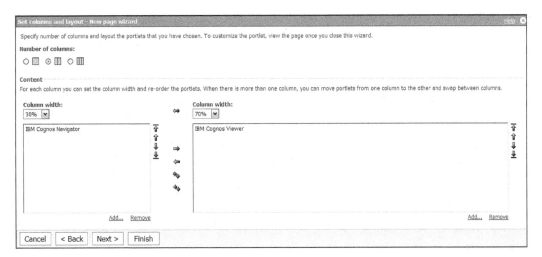

9. Click on the **Next** button to proceed to **Set page style – New page wizard**. There are options to customize the look and feel of the page. Type a title under the **Title** section and click on the **Next** button, as shown in the following screenshot:

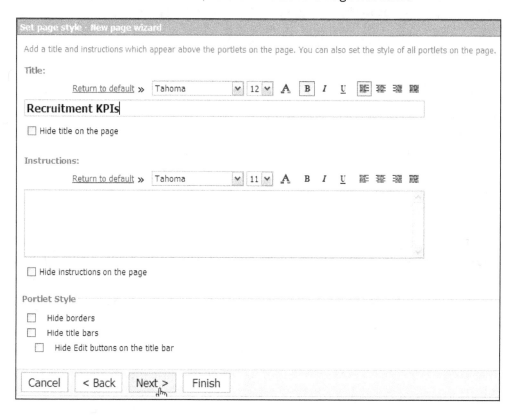

10. On the next page, select **Add this page to the portal tabs** and click on the **Finish** button, as shown in the following screenshot:

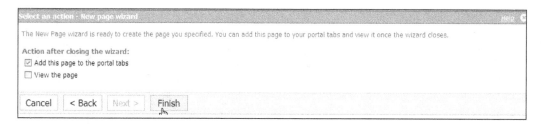

11. Notice that a new portal is added to **IBM Cognos Connection**, as shown in the following screenshot:

12. Security can be defined on this portal tab to hide or show the tab to different users, who log in and are interested to view the content on this tab. *IBM Cognos documentation* can be referred to for detailed steps needed to apply security and is beyond the scope of this book.

13. Now we want to place some Cognos content on this tab, which we want to share across users. Click on the **Recruitment KPIs** tab and notice that currently it is showing only default content, as shown in the following screenshot:

14. Click on the **Home** icon denoted by 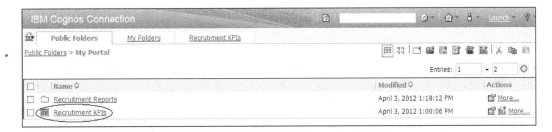 to return to **Public Folders**. Navigate to **Public Folders | My Portal** and create a folder with the name **Recruitment Reports**. Note the entry representing the newly added **Recruitment KPIs** tab. This tab can be viewed by clicking on the entry.

15. Navigate to **Public Folders | Samples | Models | GO Data Warehouse (query) | Business Insight Source Reports**, copy the **Recruitment Data** and **Recruitment Success** reports, and paste them at **Public Folders | My Portal | Recruitment Reports**.

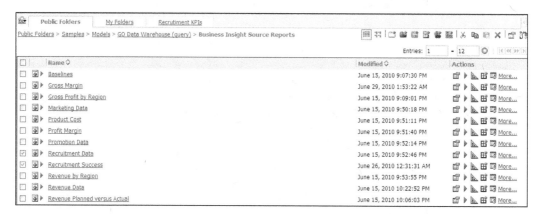

16. Similarly, go to **Public Folders | Samples | Models | GO Data Warehouse (analysis) | Report Studio Report Samples** and copy **Planned Headcount**, **Positions to fill**, and **Recruitment Report** to **Public Folders | My Portal | Recruitment Reports**. Hence, now we have copied five reports showing **Recruitment KPIs** in various formats to the folder, as shown in the following screenshot:

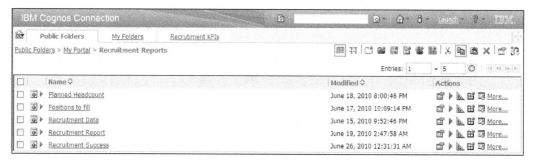

17. Now open the **Recruitment KPIs** tab and click on the **Edit** icon denoted by ▥ in the left-hand side pane, as shown in the following screenshot:

18. It will open the **Set the properties – IBM Cognos Navigator** page on which we can set various options for the **IBM Cognos Navigator** portlet, which is placed in the left-hand side pane. Change the title of the portlet by typing **Recruitment Reports** under the **Title** section, as shown in the following screenshot:

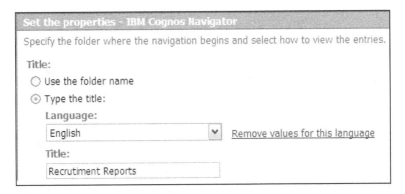

19. Set the **Folder** section to **Cognos | Public Folders | My Portal | Recruitment Reports** by clicking on the **Select a folder...** link. This enables us to select a folder on Cognos Connection, which has all the reports we want to display in the portlet.

20. Here we want to display five reports that we have copied to the **Recruitment Reports** folder in the portlet, hence we have selected the location of the folder by clicking on the **Select a folder...** link, as shown in the following screenshot:

> Folder:
>
> 🗁 Cognos > Public Folders > My Portal > Recruitment Reports
>
> <u>Select a folder...</u>

21. In the **Open links** section, select the **In a destination portlet** checkbox and type **A** for The channel name given to the **IBM Cognos Viewer** portlet. This will allow for the report output to appear only in the named portlet:

> Open links:
>
> ○ In a new browser window
> ○ In the current window
> ○ In a named HTML frame:
> [   ]
> ◉ In a destination portlet:
> The channel name given to the IBM Cognos Viewer.
> [A   ]

22. Click on the **OK** button to return to the **Recruitment KPIs** tab. Notice the change in the content which is now made available in the **IBM Cognos Navigator** portlet:

23. Similarly, click on the **Edit** icon denoted by [edit icon] for the **IBM Cognos Viewer** portlet, which is placed in the right-hand side pane.

24. For the **Title** section on the **Set the properties – IBM Cognos Viewer** page, select the **Use the entry name** checkbox, as shown in the following screenshot:

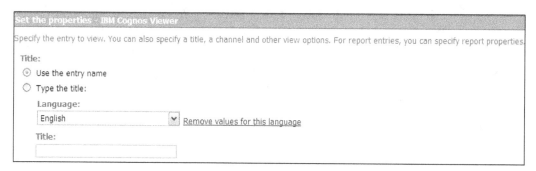

25. For the **Entry** section, select the **Planned Headcount** report, as shown in the following screenshot. This will specify the default report, which will be shown inside the portlet when the user first navigates to the tab.

26. Specify the channel name for the portlet as **A** under the **Channel** section. This should be same as what we had specified for the destination portlet while setting properties for the **IBM Cognos Navigator** portlet being displayed in the left-hand side pane.

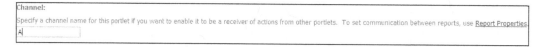

27. Click on the **OK** button to return to the **Recruitment KPIs** tab. Note the change in the view. The **Planned Headcount** report is executed and is shown on the right-hand side panel:

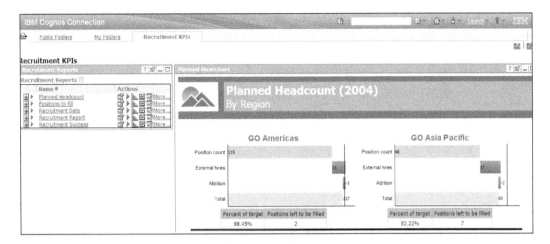

28. Users can view different reports by selecting an entry on the left-hand side panel. For instance, let us now select the **Recruitment Data** report and see how the view changes in **IBM Cognos Viewer**, as shown in the following screenshot:

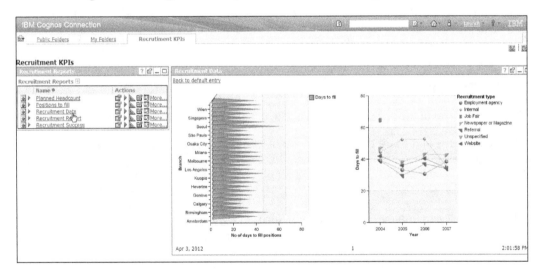

How it works...

We saw how custom portal pages can be created and added to the portal tabs. Cognos content can be placed on these portal pages in the required format and layout.

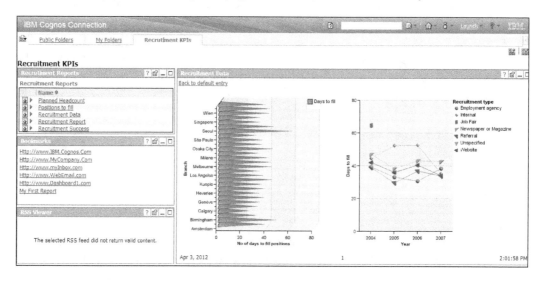

These portal tabs are made available to other users, who log on to the system and are unaware of the directory structure. They can directly click on the tabs and view the data.

Different types of content can be added to the portal tabs, which include RSS feeds, images, bookmarks, and HTML. Different portlets are available to be inserted on the tab for different content.

The look and feel of the portal tabs can also be customized according to user preferences.

Users can create and share the Cognos content with other users. Multiple portals can be created and added as portal tabs, each catering to a certain business function. Security can be defined on these portal tabs to ensure that only users from a particular business function can view these tabs.

Report authors and analysts can create and publish Cognos content to relevant portals, which can be used as a central place to share the related reports, dashboards, and views across different users.

In the next recipe we will focus on how different reports can be added as different tabs on Cognos Connection. This is another way of sharing Cognos content and it is helpful when there is a single report published with different views, each showing data for a different department or a business function.

Sharing Cognos content – adding reports as portal tabs

In the previous recipe we saw how a portal page can be designed and Cognos content can be placed on it to share it with other users.

In this recipe we will look at another way of sharing data. Here, we want to add certain reports as individual portal tabs, each of which should quickly provide a pigeon-hole view on a certain business area.

Getting ready

Make sure that IBM Cognos 10 server is up and running along with the GO Sales and GO Data Warehouse samples. Log on to Cognos Connection.

How to do it...

To add reports as portal tabs, perform the following steps:

1. In the **IBM Cognos Connection** window, navigate to **Public Folders | My Portal** and create a new folder with the name **Potal Tab Reports**, as shown in the following screenshot:

2. Navigate to **Public Folders | Samples | Models | GO Data Warehouse (query) | Business Insight Source Reports** and copy the **Revenue Data**, **Marketing Data**, and **Promotion Data** reports.

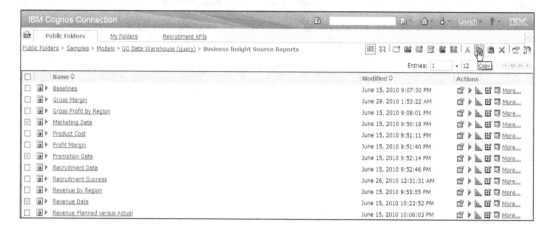

3. Paste these reports to **Public Folders | My Portal | Potal Tab Reports**, as shown in the following screenshot:

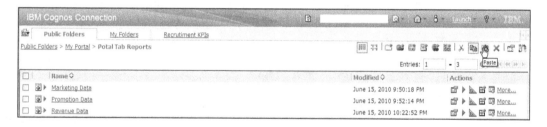

4. Now we want to have three different portal tabs for each of these reports. This will allow users to log on to Cognos Connection and view data regarding different subject areas directly in one place without navigating too much.

5. Let us now navigate to **Public Folders | My Portal** and click on the **New Page** icon denoted by 🖼 to create a new page.

6. In the **Specify a name and description – New page wizard** window, specify the name of the portal as **Executive Portal** under the **Name** section. Click on the **Next** button.

7. On the next page, keep **Number of columns** as default:

Set columns and layout - New page wizard

Specify number of columns and layout the portlets that you have chosen. To customize the portlet, view the page once you close this wizard.

Number of columns:

⊙ ▢   ○ ▢▢   ○ ▢▢▢

8. In the **Content** section, click on the **Add...** link to display the list of available portlet types, as shown in the following screenshot:

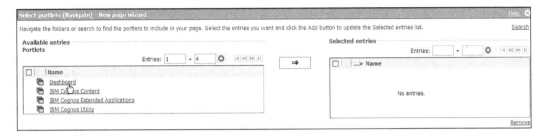

9. Click on **Dashboard** and select the **Multi-page** template, as shown in the following screenshot:

10. Click on **OK** to come back to the **Set columns and layout – New page wizard** page, as shown in the following screenshot:

11. Click on the **Next** button. This will now open the **Set page style** page.

12. Specify the title as **Executive Dashboard** under the **Title** section and click on the **Next** button.

13. On the **Select an action – New page wizard** page, select the **Add this page to the portal tabs** checkbox, as shown in the following screenshot:

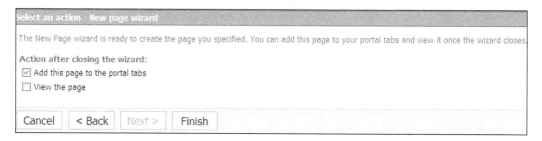

14. Click on the **Finish** button to return to **IBM Cognos Connection**. A separate portal called **Executive Portal** is now available. Click on the tab and it is now possible to insert Cognos content.

15. Click on the **Edit** icon denoted by 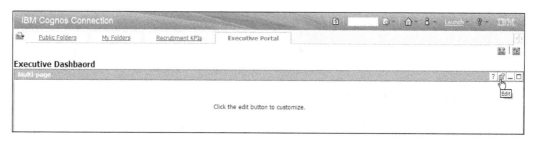, as shown in the following screenshot:

16. This will open **Set the properties – Multi-page**, which allows the user to configure the **Multi-page** portal.

17. Change **Title** to **Executive Dashboard**. Under the Folder section, click on **Select an entry...** to navigate to **Public Folders | My Portal** and select the **Portal Tab Reports** folder, as shown in the following screenshot:

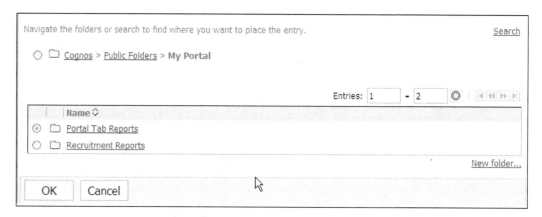

18. Keep the rest of the options set to default and click on the **OK** button.

Set the properties - Multi-page

Specify the folder to use as the source of entries and select the display style. You can also specify a title and other view options

Title:

○ Use the folder name

◉ Type the title:

Language:

| English ▾ | Remove values for this language |

Title:

| Executive Dashboard |

Folder:

☐ Cognos > Public Folders > My Portal > Portal Tab Reports

Select an entry... Clear

---

19. Click on the **Executive Portal** tab, which will now show three subtabs, each showing the report we had placed in the **Portal Tab Reports** folder, as shown in the following screenshot:

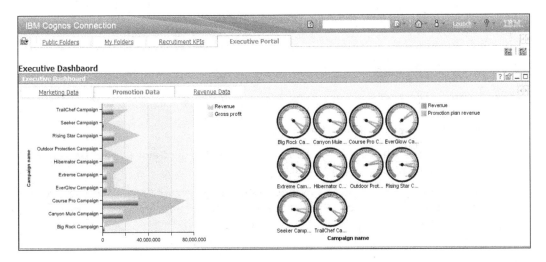

20. A user can log on to **IBM Cognos Connection** and depending on the security settings can view any of the subtabs under **Executive Portal**. He/she doesn't have to be bothered about which sources the data is coming from onto the dashboard. The user just needs to click on **Marketing Data**, **Promotion Data**, or **Revenue Data** to view the dashboard relevant to his/her area of interest.

How it works...

In this recipe we saw another way of sharing data across users. If this is clubbed with appropriate security settings, it will make sure that the relevant data is shared only with a corresponding set of users.

The next recipe will focus on making dashboards created in IBM Cognos Business Insight available to users, so that these can be shared and collaborated on.

Sharing the IBM Cognos Business Insight dashboard

In this recipe we will learn how we can create a portal page based on an existing dashboard created in IBM Cognos Business Insight.

This would help users to share dashboards that they created in IBM Cognos Business Insight, with other users by placing them on a portal page.

Getting ready

Make sure that IBM Cognos 10 BI server is started. The GO Sales and GO Data Warehouse samples should be set up and working. Log on to **IBM Cognos Connection**.

How to do it...

To share the IBM Cognos Business Insight dashboard, perform the following steps:

1. Navigate to **Public Folders | My Portal**.

2. Click on the ⊞ icon to create a new page. We want to put **Sales by Year Dashboard** shipped with samples on the portal page.

3. On the **Specify a name and description – New page wizard** page, specify **Name** as **Sales Dashboard**. Click on the **Next** button, as shown in the following screenshot:

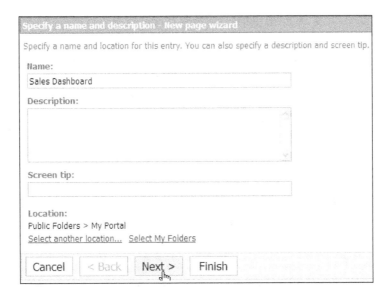

4. On the **Set columns and layout – New page wizard** page, keep the **Number of columns** option set to default.

5. In the **Content** section, add the **HTML Viewer** portlet from IBM Cognos Utility, as shown in the following screenshot:

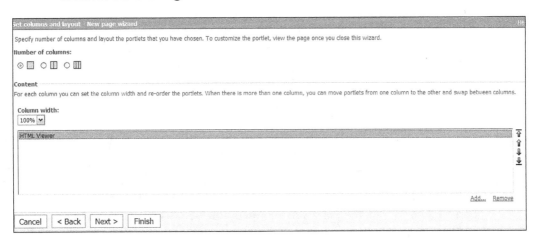

6. Click on the **Next** button.

7. On the **Set page style** page, specify the title as **Sales Dashboard** under the **Title** section and click on the **Next** button.

8. On the **Select an action** page, select the **Add this page to the portal tabs** option. Click on the **Finish** button.

9. This will navigate us back to **IBM Cognos Connection**.

10. Navigate to **Public Folders | Samples | Models | Business Insight Samples** and click on **Sales by Year Dashboard** to open it in IBM Cognos Business Insight, as shown in the following screenshot:

11. In the IBM Cognos Business Insight interface, click on the icon to expand the menu. Click on the **Copy Link to Clipboard** option, as shown in the following screenshot:

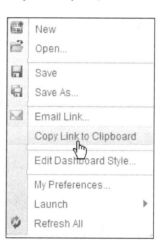

12. Paste the link in any text editor. This is the link to the dashboard that we want to place on the **Sales Dashboard** portal tab. Navigate back to **IBM Cognos Connection**. Click on the **Sales Dashboard** portal tab, which does not display anything on it for now.

13. Click on the **Edit** icon on the portal, as shown in the following screenshot:

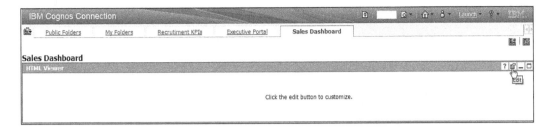

14. On the **Set the properties** page for the **HTML Viewer** portlet, under the **Title** section type **Sales Dashboard**.

15. Copy the **Sales by Year Dashboard** URL from the text editor and paste it under **HTML content**. Under the **View options** section, specify **Height (pixels)** as **900** and click on the **OK** button, as shown in the following screenshot:

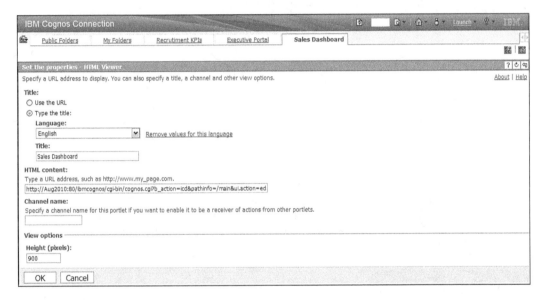

16. This will update the **Sales Dashboard** tab, as shown in the following screenshot:

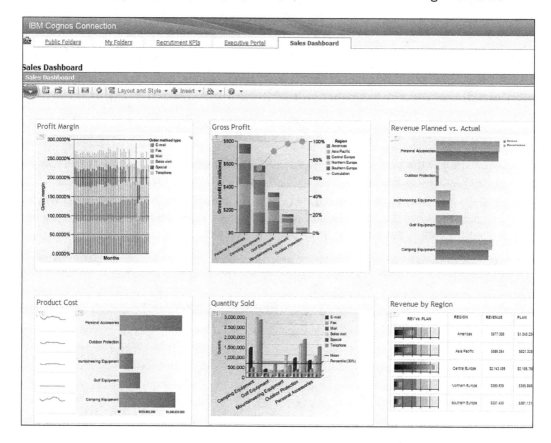

17. Hence, a user logging in to **IBM Cognos Connection** can directly click on the **Sales Dashboard** tab for sales-related information without having to navigate to the actual source file.

How it works...

In the preceding sections we saw how users can add Cognos content on portal pages. This enables users to share and collaborate with other users as required.

Index

Thank you for buying
IBM Cognos Business Intelligence 10.1
Dashboarding Cookbook

About Packt Publishing

Packt, pronounced 'packed', published its first book "*Mastering phpMyAdmin for Effective MySQL Management*" in April 2004 and subsequently continued to specialize in publishing highly focused books on specific technologies and solutions.

Our books and publications share the experiences of your fellow IT professionals in adapting and customizing today's systems, applications, and frameworks. Our solution-based books give you the knowledge and power to customize the software and technologies you're using to get the job done. Packt books are more specific and less general than the IT books you have seen in the past. Our unique business model allows us to bring you more focused information, giving you more of what you need to know, and less of what you don't.

Packt is a modern, yet unique publishing company, which focuses on producing quality, cutting-edge books for communities of developers, administrators, and newbies alike. For more information, please visit our website: www.PacktPub.com.

About Packt Enterprise

In 2010, Packt launched two new brands, Packt Enterprise and Packt Open Source, in order to continue its focus on specialization. This book is part of the Packt Enterprise brand, home to books published on enterprise software – software created by major vendors, including (but not limited to) IBM, Microsoft and Oracle, often for use in other corporations. Its titles will offer information relevant to a range of users of this software, including administrators, developers, architects, and end users.

Writing for Packt

We welcome all inquiries from people who are interested in authoring. Book proposals should be sent to author@packtpub.com. If your book idea is still at an early stage and you would like to discuss it first before writing a formal book proposal, contact us; one of our commissioning editors will get in touch with you.

We're not just looking for published authors; if you have strong technical skills but no writing experience, our experienced editors can help you develop a writing career, or simply get some additional reward for your expertise.

IBM Cognos TM1 Developer's Certification guide

ISBN: 978-1-849684-90-3   Paperback: 240 pages

Fast track your way to COG-310 certification!

IBM Cognos TM1 Developer's Certification Guide

Fast track your way to COG-310 certification!

James D. Miller

1. Successfully clear COG-310 certification.

2. Master the major components that make up Cognos TM1 and learn the function of each.

3. Understand the advantages of using Rules versus Turbo Integrator

4. This book provides a perfect study outline and self-test for each exam topic

---

IBM Cognos TM1 Cookbook

ISBN: 978-1-849682-10-7   Paperback: 490 pages

Build real world planning, budgeting, and forecasting solutions with a collection of over 60 simple but incredibly effective recipes

IBM Cognos TM1 Cookbook

Build real world planning, budgeting, and forecasting solutions with a collection of over 60 simple but incredibly effective recipes

Ankit Garg

1. A comprehensive developer's guide for planning, building, and managing practical applications with IBM TM1

2. No prior knowledge of TM1 expected

3. Complete coverage of all the important aspects of IBM TM1 in carefully planned step-by-step practical demos

4. Part of Packt's Cookbook series: Practical recipes that illustrate the use of various TM1 features

Please check **www.PacktPub.com** for information on our titles

IBM Cognos 8 Report Studio Cookbook

ISBN: 978-1-849680-34-9   Paperback: 252 pages

Over 80 great receipes for taking control of Cognos 8 Report Studio

1. Learn advanced techniques to produce real-life reports that meet business demands

2. Tricks and hacks for speedy and effortless report development and to overcome tool-based limitations

3. Peek into the best practices used in industry and discern ways to work like a pro

4. Part of Packt's Cookbook series-each recipe is a carefully organized sequence of instructions to complete the task as efficiently as possible

IBM Cognos 8 Planning

ISBN: 978-1-847196-84-2   Paperback: 424 pages

A practical guide to developing and deploying planning models for your enterprise

1. Build and deploy effective planning models using Cognos 8 Planning

2. Filled with ideas and techniques for designing planning models

3. Ample screenshots and clear explanations to facilitate learning

4. Written for first-time developers focusing on what is important to the beginner

5. A step-by-step approach that will help you strengthen your understanding of all the major concepts

Please check **www.PacktPub.com** for information on our titles

www.ingramcontent.com/pod-product-compliance
Lightning Source LLC
LaVergne TN
LVHW062316060326
832902LV00013B/2245